"Dr. Thomas A. Richards' therapy series is an excellent resource to use with clients suffering from social anxiety disorder. I have found it to provide direct solutions to the vexing problem of this disorder. There is no book anywhere that contains the valuable lessons that are included in "Overcoming Social Anxiety: Step by Step."

-- Javier Ballesteros, Psy.D.
Licensed Clinical Psychologist, New York State

"I've used Dr. Richards' therapy series "Overcoming Social Anxiety: Step by Step" with my clients for the past 14 years. The therapy sessions and book handouts have been healing and life changing for countless numbers of people. I have witnessed this first hand in the many comprehensive CBT groups I have offered.

I've found the handouts to be an outstanding client resource, and have been excited watching people learn to overcome social anxiety one step at a time. Beyond that, I have personally benefited from these great materials too."

-- Richard A. Preuit, M.A., LMFT
Arcadia, California

"Using Dr. Richards' therapy series in conjunction with a cognitive behavioral therapy group for social anxiety was life changing for me. The handouts were a key component in helping me to overcome social anxiety. I continue to use some of the key concepts from the handouts with my daily inner dialogue. I've had many experiences with Dr. Richards' programs since 2001; from going through the therapy myself to using it as part of a treatment approach to help others in my own private practice. I feel the therapy program was essential in helping me to overcome social anxiety."

-- Dr. Jason Buck, LPC
Doctor of Behavioral Health, Arizona
Desert Eagle Counseling Services, PLLC

Comments from users of the "Overcoming Social Anxiety: Step by Step" therapy program by Dr. Thomas A. Richards

I feel like I can only get better now, and I definitely plan on keeping all the skills I've learned from your series for the rest of my life, so that I can have a better one.

-- Marc B. Andrews

BACK THEN: I felt the way things were going in my life were hopeless. I didn't know what to do to get better.

NOW: Through your therapy, I have learned of the choices I have and the things to tell myself in order to feel better bit by bit. I learned I always have choices and little steps that I can take to slowly move my life in a more positive and healthier direction.

-- Robert Lanmile

I can say for once that I am starting a new year with great optimism and eagerness. New hope brings new plans. And I am pursuing them with more sureness and confidence than ever before.

-- Lisa Gordon

A year is a long time!
But wow! What a long way to come! I wouldn't have believed it 6 months ago!
-- Sarah Hemphill

Realizing that I was not the only one with this problem and it had a name – "Social Anxiety" – was the first step to recovery. Dr. Richard's cognitive therapy has completely changed my life. I am doing things I never thought I could do and I am doing them without anxiety!

-- Penelope Rodriguez

So to the people who wonder... the therapy works – but it takes repetition and reinforcement.

-- Barbara Olivetti

What I have learned from Dr. Richards' therapy series and what I appreciate even more than overcoming my social anxiety is my new outlook on life. I have a choice how I react to every situation I encounter. I am in control of my thoughts and feelings – I find this so comforting and yet so very powerful.

-- Wendy Grayson

Dear Dr. Richards,

Your program has brought me hope and help. Working through the series has given me tools for managing and minimizing my SAD. The structured approach provided by your series has been essential to my progress in overcoming social anxiety.

-- Cynthia Minmisser

Fortunately, Dr. Richards' series gave me hope that I could change and that I could eventually form other relationships, and this hope helped me get through this painful period.

The series also gave me the inspiration to return to school to work on a master's degree. I had wanted to do this for years, but my anxiety held me back.

-- Tyler Stark

Dr. Richards' therapy series helped me turn the tables on my ANTs and gave me the confidence to believe in myself. The messages echoed in the sessions and in the workbook reinforced the revolutionary (for me) idea that I was actually a good person – someone who was entitled to friendship, companionship and (gasp!) even love!

-- Gerry O'Ryan

Your therapy series on "Overcoming Social Anxiety" pulls together in one package helpful information and validates the ongoing cognitive work I have been doing in years past. I'm a person who just knows when something feels right, rings true, and when it comes to self-help, I need this believing to put recommendations into action. I feel very rooted in your work, and am very, very grateful that I discovered your program.

-- Janice Schultz

It's now been over a year and a half since I started your program and my life has totally changed. I have stopped running from my fears and have learned to accept who I am.

THANK YOU FOR ALLOWING ME TO TAKE CONTROL OF MY LIFE!

-- Jason Nebring

I woke up this morning, energized, motivated and WITHOUT feeling anxiety. I've woken up to anxiety every morning for the past 15 years. I cannot put into words how free I felt this morning.

-- Noah Daniels

I have been in individual counseling for several years and no one has impressed upon me WHY I should be doing the cognitive therapy as you have explained. I know I am not done, and have many areas still to work on, but I feel so much better already! I think it's because not only do I now have hope, but I know that I can and will get better.

Now I understand why you keep saying "Start your therapy today." I would still be an anxious mess if I hadn't done something about it. Thank you again.

-- Marlene Timari

Completing the "Overcoming Social Anxiety" therapy series changed my life. After doing the therapy I am able to attend university, after several years of avoiding school. I feel less anxious and self-conscious being in a classroom with other students, and I have been able to answer and ask questions in class while experiencing very little anxiety.

I know that I would not have been able to do these things if it wasn't for the therapy series.

-- Mike Whritenour

Not everything in my life is perfect, I'm still changing and evolving, but it's nice to be changing in a positive direction and to have the tools that affect change in unhealthy thinking patterns. I guess that's why, since CBT, I see my life as like a renaissance. Now, my path is clear and this life journey is truly wondrous. Once the momentum begins... it's boundless.

-- Emily Jackson

The good news is that the thought of introductions, presentations, meetings and group discussions don't scare me anymore. Applying the therapy has really worked. I'm happy and I deserve it.

-- Vanessa Kocurek

Therapy is the same thing we've been doing for all these years, except it makes you feel better, not worse. For the first time in years I feel like life will get better.

So to all you doubters out there unsure about the therapy, try and look at it in a different light.

-- T. J. Cleary

I feel good and enjoy challenging myself. No longer trapped being a certain type of person because of what I believed in the past and how I thought I had to behave. I am no longer a list of disorders!

This has taken time but it is so worth putting in the time. I remember you saying something about how the audio series would help people get over social anxiety, but more than that it would lead to a never ending journey of development. That has absolutely been my experience.

I read some other books while I was doing the series the second time round – one on body dysmorphic disorder for example. But it was your audio series that broke apart the prison of false neural connections and beliefs I had been trapped inside. You enabled me for the first time to see outside of the box I was in, so that I was able to believe what you were telling me.

Thank you, thank you, thank you!

My life has radically changed!!

-- Stacy K. Levinson

I have been working on the therapy series, currently starting session 13. When I listened to the first session, I cried tears of joy at finally finding someone who so thoroughly understands this disorder.

The therapy sessions and handouts are helping me to change the way I think. I have noticed a big difference in how I am handling life. I am able to do things without that constant critical voice pulling me down. I have pretty much stopped having ANTS, or I quickly catch any that try to sneak by.

-- Susan Parker

This series is the greatest thing to ever happen to me. (I waited fifteen years for something like this!)

-- Jeff M. Jeffries

Being a skeptic and a pessimist, I avoided therapy for a long time thinking it was stupid and only worked for gullible people (sorry).

I thought repeating things to myself was basically telling myself lies so I could screw reality and be happy. I thought I was too smart and that it wouldn't work for me.

But last night, I realized what potent a technique repeating things to yourself is. I realized:

That's how I got this way in the first place!

-- Todd Albright

I've learned I'm the captain of my ship and I had a choice. You can choose to feel miserable all of your days, or you can choose to make decisions today that will make your life better tomorrow.

BACK THEN – I wouldn't believe this for a second.

NOW – I am only beginning to realize what the possibilities are.

-- A.W.

On December 14, I received the therapy series and began to listen to it right away. As days went on, I felt encouraged and even happy that I finally found something that would help me change my life.

I am a logical and analytical person and it really makes sense that one needs to reprogram the brain away from the old gutter negative thinking habits that have been lodged like a dagger in the brain for years.

-- Tom McNally

I've been following the program religiously and have found the techniques to be extremely helpful.

My confidence is starting to come back and I'm starting to accept myself as well as the fact that not everyone is going to like me.

When I first received the therapy series, I was skeptical of the methods and techniques used in cognitive behavioral therapy, but now I realize the effectiveness of the treatment.

To everyone going through the therapy series, I strongly encourage you to not give up, continue with the daily exercises, and not lose hope of leading a better life. If I can do it, anyone can!

-- Will Garza

After living with this mess called social anxiety for most of my life, it was exhilarating to hear – for REAL – that there was help for me. When I began listening to the sessions, though, I still was amazed that this therapy you were talking about applied directly to me! I really couldn't (and hadn't) believed it would be so direct, and practical, and so good.

Now, after receiving this large series, and working on about half of it so far, I can tell you it was worth the wait. I really can't believe how my thinking pattern got so out of whack. I am seeing things more rationally now, even though I have a ways to go. But maybe the most important thing is that I am much more in control of my anxiety than ever before. I can feel this and I feel like shouting every day from happiness!

My anxiety used to eat away at me constantly. But the therapy, which I knew I had to apply and apply to my own life, has already made a big difference.

I don't want you to think I'm prefect or "recovered" yet, but I am amazed at the amount of progress I have made in the last two months.

I could say a lot more, but I wanted to thank you, and whoever else is involved, for this therapy series. It really is just made for social anxiety, and I can tell you know what to do because you suffered from social anxiety most all your life.

-- Dan Bateman

Table of Contents

Title Page	13
Dedication	14
Introduction to the Series	15
The Brain	17
Cognitive Behavioral Therapy	18
How and When to Practice	19
Slow Talk	21
Slow Thinking	25
Catch, Label, and Tell Your Brain the Truth	27
Distraction Suggestions	29
The ANTs Handout	31
The Annual ANTs Convention	35
Rational Coping Statements	39
Neurons that Fire Together, Wire Together	41
The Joys of Beating Myself Up	45
Attitudes	47
The "Look Around Technique"	51
Setbacks Happen to Everyone	55
A "Balance Sheet" for Facing Anxiety	59
The Fighting Paradox	63
Bears Attack & Maul, Bees Swarm & Sting	69
Don't Feed Anxiety: Let it Starve and Disappear	71
Einstein's Definition of "Insanity"	73
Loosen Up and Let Stress Go	75
How to Temporarily Cut Down on Feelings of Anxiety	79
Accepting Myself As I Am Right Now	81
Choose the Easiest Way to Begin Behavioral Therapy	83
The Phenomenal Power of One Little Drop of Water	87
Progressive Muscle Relaxation	89
Replacing ANTs Thoughts with Automatic Rational Thinking (ART)	93
Turning the Tables on the ANTs, Part I	95
De-Stressing Strategies	101
Quick PMR	103
Turning the Tables on the ANTs, Part II	105
Go Conditional With Your Thoughts and Beliefs	111
Are You on the Right Track With Your Comprehensive CBT?	115
Cognitive Distortions	117
Small Talk is "Small Talk" Because it's Small	121
Turning the Tables on the ANTs, Part III	125
The Social Anxiety "Automatic" Cycle	127
How You See Yourself and the World, Part I	131

Funny Stuff is Great Medicine Against Social Anxiety	135
If You Firmly Believe Something	137
The Brain Recycles (and recycles) What We Already Believe	141
How You See Yourself and the World, Part II	143
We Are Always Doing "Therapy" on Ourselves	147
"I Can't Do It" Thinking	149
Beginning Behavioral Activities	153
Suggestions for Putting Cognitive Therapy into Place	155
Setbacks: Two Competing Neural Pathways in Your Brain	157
Keep Your Brain Open to New Interpretations	161
How You See Yourself and the World, Part III	165
Behavioral Activities, Part II	169
Active Listening, External Focusing, and Taking the Initiative	173
Vicious Circles and How to Shrink Them	179
Mingling	183
The Deserving Statements	189
Perfectionism and Pressure	191
External Focusing	195
How to Be More Assertive	199
How to Be Calm and Assertive: An Example	201
Reducing Self-Consciousness	205
Brainwashing	209
The Profound Concept	211
Making Conversations	215
Should We Be Living in a Hostile World?	219
The Good, the Better, and the Beautiful	223
Act Against Your Negative Feelings	225
The Power Statements	229
Behavioral Experiments: Staying in the Moment	233
Self-Statements: Moving in a Positive Direction	237
Avoidance: Our Worst Enemy	239
Irrational Expectations Are Killers	241
Have a Rational Talk With Yourself Every Day	245
Poisonous Thoughts	247
Worry… Leads to More Worry and More Worry	251
Feelings, Feelings, and More Feelings	253
Shyness, Timidity, and Being Hesitant	257
Therapy Strategies That Seem Small, But Have Really Powerful Results	261
Seeing Things from a Different Perspective	263
Stay Out of the Twilight Zone, Move into the "Peace Zone"	267
Acceptance is an Active Experience	269
Seeing the Present	273
At the Crossroads	275
Letting Go of the Negative Past	279

Taking Responsibility and Making Choices	283
Be Honest With Yourself	285
Improving our Public Speaking, Presentations, and Talks	287
The Perfectionism Pit	291
Eliminating Fear and Anxiety Permanently: Taking the Last Step	293
The Paradox of the Rain	297
Keep the Momentum Going and Do Not Give Up	299
Where To Go for More Information	303
About Dr. Richards and the Social Anxiety Institute	305

All rights reserved.
2014 copyright, Thomas A. Richards
No part of this book may be reproduced or transmitted in any form or by any means, electronic or mechanical, including photocopying, recording, or any type of information storage and retrieval system, without permission from the Social Anxiety Institute Press.

Library of Congress Cataloging in Publication Data
Thomas A. Richards.
    Overcoming Social Anxiety: Step by Step / Thomas A. Richards
Includes index
ISBN-13: 978-1497584563
ISBN-10: 1497584566

1. Social Anxiety Disorder 2. Cognitive-Behavioral Therapy

Published simultaneously world-wide by the Social Anxiety Institute Press.

Printed in the United States of America.

Editorial Assistance: Justin Bashore, Aaron O'Banion, Matthew Whitley

Cover Design: Zach Brown

Photos ©Istock.com

ISBN-13: 978-1497584563

ISBN-10: 1497584566

©2014, The Social Anxiety Institute, Inc. Thomas A. Richards, Ph.D.
This material may not be reproduced or redistributed in any fashion.

Overcoming Social Anxiety:
Step By Step

Thomas A. Richards, Ph.D.,

Psychologist/Director, The Social Anxiety Institute, Inc.

This book contains the handouts accompanying the new, updated audio video therapy series "Overcoming Social Anxiety: Step By Step."

©2014, The Social Anxiety Institute, Inc. Thomas A. Richards, Ph.D.
This material may not be reproduced or redistributed in any fashion.

Dedication

This therapy series is dedicated to:

Lionel E. (1895-1968) and Pearl M. Jones (1896-1981), my maternal grandparents, who were always loyal, caring, and loving.

Gerry Walsh Platteter (1919-2011), my aunt, who stayed active until her death.

Marilyn Jane Connelly (1935-1996), an especially kind and special person, and

Justin Bashore, who has worked on this and several other projects since their inception, helping in any way he could.

Introduction to the New Audio Video Therapy Series

The **Social Anxiety Institute's** website (http://socialanxietyinstitute.org) was the first internet site to explain and thoroughly detail social anxiety disorder when it went live in the 1990s. Dr. Richards was the only psychologist speaking directly from his own experience of working to help people with social anxiety get better. We were at the beginning of our group therapy program at that time, and the first groups of people were learning how to overcome social anxiety.

In 1996, we began receiving hundreds of e-mails a week from people who had just discovered what they were suffering from, and wanted a way out. We saw the demographic data indicating that 7% of the population suffered from social anxiety disorder, but we still weren't ready for the outpouring of need we received from all over the world.

Over a period of several years, as Dr. Richards worked with local therapy groups, we researched how and what to include in the initial series. The first series, in audio format only, was published in 2000, and there were several minor revisions of the audio series during the next ten years. It's estimated that over 25,000 people used the audio series to help them reduce their social anxiety.

Because the Social Anxiety Institute remains the only place in the world that runs cognitive-behavioral programs for people with social anxiety, we took what we had learned over the past twenty years and rewrote the entire series, adding to it where necessary, eliminating less important material, and trying to integrate the cognitive strategies with the behavioral activities as much as possible. The therapy is now in audio and video components and has a large amount of supplemental material accompanying it online, including extra handouts, songs, videos, diagrams, and a private forum for developing an online community.

Our hope is that this new series will be used by millions of people with social anxiety disorder, as they begin learning the cognitive strategies that will help them get better. The brain's plasticity is amazing, and you can learn to think, believe, and feel rationally, instead of letting anxiety cripple your life.

That is the purpose of this therapy series.

To access the new audio/video therapy series, go here:

http://members.socialanxietyinstitute.org

You can sign up to use the new therapy series "Overcoming Social Anxiety: Step by Step" by going to the institute's website:

http://socialanxietyinstitute.org

Overcoming social anxiety is the most important thing you can do right now for yourself. Take the time, patiently learn the cognitive strategies, and allow your brain to change its thoughts, beliefs, and feelings, so that you can become an entirely new person, free from the restrictions that social anxiety causes.

The Brain

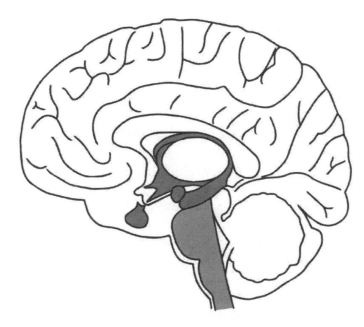

The Brain

The brain weighs about three pounds and its texture is similar to jelly.

The **top part** of the brain, in white, called the cerebrum, is where our brain processes information: our thinking, planning, remembering, and perceiving. We also call this the *cognitive brain*. This is where the new strategies, methods, and concepts we learn will be processed so that our brains gradually change, and our new habits become "automatic."

The **middle part** of the brain is the mid-region part of the brain and is sometimes referred to as the "limbic system." This region of the brain, for our purposes, processes emotions and can be called the *emotional brain*. It controls *all* of our emotions – the negative ones, such as anxiety, fear, depression, irritation, frustration, and anger – and also the positive emotions, such as peace, happiness, humor, enjoyment, contentment, and calmness.

The **brainstem** (in gray) sits on top of the spinal column, and keeps you alive (i.e., through its involuntary activities, such as regulating heartbeat and breathing.)

Cognitive-Behavioral Therapy

We need to deal with anxiety and depression from every therapeutic angle that we have available to us. Cognitive-behavioral therapy specific to social anxiety has been shown to be most effective, as it literally *changes* the brain. Therefore, we focus on three main areas:

1. COGNITIVE	2. BEHAVIORAL	3. EMOTIONAL
(thinking/belief processes)	(our actions/what we do)	(emotional brain strategies)
We learn new methods to change our old thinking patterns and habits.	The behavioral aspect of therapy is the part where we actually put everything into place in everyday, real-life situations.	It is important to learn to control our emotions. A type of calming strategy should be accessible to everyone. The feelings of calmness and peace are emphasized and allowed to grow.
We have several dozen MAJOR strategies that we use to reduce anxiety.	This area is best handled along with cognitive therapy, because we need a strong foundation of cognitive and emotional skills/strategies so that we can begin living and acting differently.	The more your brain is quiet and relaxed, the easier therapeutic information can be processed. Being calm allows the therapy to reach your brain and be understood better.
Strategies Useful to Changing Negative Thoughts:		
Slow-talk (Calm talk),		
Negative thought stoppage,	Behavioral treatment is essential. We must put the cognitive methods and strategies we learn into practice.	*Strategies to become more emotionally rational:*
Changing irrational beliefs into rational beliefs,		"The Peace zone,"
The "fighting" paradox,		Determined slow /calm talk,
Rational self-talk,	We put cognitive methods into behavioral practice in a step by step, hierarchical way, starting from what is least anxiety-causing, and working our way up, incrementally, from that point.	Imaging,
Moving our self-statements up,		Progressive muscle relaxation,
Assertiveness,		
Correction of cognitive distortions,		Meditation,
A rational view of the world and how we fit into it		Mindfulness
		Other Relaxation Methods

How and When to Practice

1. It is important that you become familiar with the strategies you're learning before you start using them in real-life situations. Therefore, when a strategy or method is being learned and is new to you, it's always best to practice it when you're feeling relatively calm, and when you're alone by yourself, to prevent any kind of self-consciousness. We suggest at least thirty minutes a day of reading the relevant handouts over to yourself, to give them a chance to be learned by the brain.

Don't feel overwhelmed by the therapy. Relax and take your time.

2. The therapy you're learning does not need to be beat into the ground the first week. Take a determined, yet gentle, approach to it. Thirty minutes a day (which can be split up if necessary) is necessary but adequate. You get better results by doing therapy in the morning when your brain is fresh, and by reinforcing the therapy throughout the day: at breaks, lunch, or when you get home. Later, we'll talk about how you can reinforce the therapy while you're at work or school – without anyone else even knowing what you're doing. I will give you guidelines about what to do during the week at the end of every session.

3. Reading over the handouts out loud to yourself every day is the best way to keep reminding your brain what you're doing. This, of course, allows the therapy to sink in to your brain a little more deeply each time. When your eyes read the message, and your ears hear the sound vibrations, the brain takes it all in, and sends it to different areas of the brain. Because of this, you are hitting tens of millions more brain cells. Reading the handouts out loud to yourself allows progress to happen faster, because you are using more neurons in your brain to process the information.

4. Cognitive-behavioral therapy works best for anxiety disorders. Research and clinical experience alike consistently indicate that comprehensive cognitive-

behavioral therapy for social anxiety is life-changing. Repetition and persistence with the methods and strategies that make permanent changes in the brain helps us overcome social anxiety.

5. If we want a permanent change in our brain – and we do – we must *practice* and be *persistent*. The brain cannot be changed overnight. Overcoming social anxiety is a process that takes patience and time to occur. We must do therapy in the way the human brain processes our words and deeds. We can't force the brain to believe things it hasn't had the time to process adequately. Our actions must correlate with the way the brain works physiologically, so that therapy has a permanent effect on our lives.

6. Contrary to popular thought, medication does not permanently change "brain chemistry." It may temporarily help, if the medication calms you down and helps you do the cognitive-behavioral therapy. The drug, however, is not "curing" you. The only way to permanently change neural pathways in the brain is by doing active CBT so that your brain (i.e., you) think, believe, and feel differently.

7. Do the therapy when you are calm and relaxed. Your brain takes in the strategies better when you are relaxed and calm. If you're agitated and anxious, the brain is not going to focus on the therapy you might try to do. It is important to be relaxed first -- before you do the therapy.

So, if you're feeling anxious, depressed, agitated, or any other negative emotion, burn off that excessive adrenaline and cortisol by:

   a. Exercising for twenty to thirty minutes.
   b. Singing along to your favorite (positive) music.
   c. Talking to a friend who is positive and supports you.
   d. Relaxing, meditating, or listening to peaceful music or sounds.
   e. Anything at all that helps you to calm down and relax, so that you can be relatively calm and peaceful during your 30 minute therapy time.

It takes consistent repetition before your brain starts to automatically use these strategies.

Slow Talk

Slow talk is helpful and practical because it slows our physiological responses down. Using slow talk calms our rapid heartbeat, our rising blood pressure, and fear of impending danger. We calm down the excess adrenaline and cortisol in our bodies when we use slow talk. It enables us to feel more relaxed and less anxious. We can use slow talk to accomplish all this.

By using slow talk, we keep the rhythm of our speaking at a regular pace, rather than speeding up and letting anxiety take control.

In the past, anxiety caused us to speed up, our thoughts went a hundred miles an hour, and we felt overwhelmed because of it. Too much was happening… too fast.

When we feel anxious, *adrenaline* has pushed us so far that the brain is overwhelmed with negative thoughts and emotions, and we are unable to slow things down and be rational. Some people freeze when the automatic negative thoughts are this racy. Others try to speak, and end up saying something forced, quick, and out of context.

Sometimes we make no sense because we mumble and stammer under our breath. In the race to say something and get it over with, we pressure ourselves to say anything, whether it makes sense or not.

Responding to anxiety by speeding up is a recipe for disaster – not a solution to the problem.

Slow talk is simply talking slowly and calmly. There is nothing magical about it. All that's involved is relaxing – to prevent yourself from speeding up. You use slow talk to keep yourself away from the rush of anxiety and the damage it causes.

By deliberately taking your time and slowing yourself down, you'll be slowing down the excessive rush of adrenaline and cortisol in your body. Keeping your speech at a regular steady rhythm, and not allowing anxiety to speed you up, will reduce the amount of anxiety you feel and allow you to be calmer.

Slow talk takes the pressure off yourself, and returns you to a calmer frame of mind. As you speak in slow talk, you begin to control the excessive release of adrenaline and cortisol in your body.

Slow talk or calm talk means just that. When we are talking, we are not going to speed up. Even when we feel anxious, we speak calmly, peacefully, and clearly, and we take our time.

If we speed up, as anxiety wants us to do, we start to think and talk very quickly. The faster we think, the more runaway our thoughts become, and our brain is filled with anxiety and fear.

We need to slow down and calm down instead. The quickest way to do that is by slowing our speaking down.

Slowing the speed of your talking when you feel anxious slows the excessive adrenaline being released. It relaxes you, calms you, and clears your mind – all at the same time. With practice, you will feel the difference, as you deliberately refuse to be pressured and rushed into things.

Relax, and give yourself enough time to respond to the situation. By refusing to rush yourself, your mind stays calm and organized.

When you speak in slow talk, you sound clear and understandable. You sound more organized and focused. In return, people hear what you're saying as being valuable – because slowing down – and not rushing things – sounds more professional and authoritative.

Physiologically, by refusing to speed up, you are not allowing the adrenal glands to flood your body with excessive amounts of adrenaline and cortisol.

Just like it sounds, slow talk is nothing more than slowing down your speech so that the adrenaline and cortisol in your body is slowed down, too. When you take your time, refuse to speed up, and use slow talk, your heart rate and blood pressure both go down.

We want to use slow talk to calm ourselves down – with our speech, and with all our other physical responses as well.

Eventually, our body slows down because we have practiced using slow talk until it's second nature to us. By slowing or calming down, you put yourself in *control* of your emotions.

When you want to control anxiety, the first thing you do is slow yourself down, and if you're in a social situation, you slow your speech down. By doing this, it puts you in control of your anxiety. As you use slow talk more often and in more situations, it becomes routine and becomes a habit. Then you have a strategy that can always keep anxiety away.

The greatest benefit of all is that you feel *less anxious*. You have some control over your anxiety.

As you talk to others or read something over to yourself in slow talk, you sound more relaxed and peaceful. You *feel* this calmness, and the clarity of thought you bring to the conversation is *heard* by other people.

As a result, other people feel comfortable in your presence. They feel relaxed around you. All of this happens as a result of slowing yourself down by using slow talk.

By using slow talk, you are calming down your social anxiety.

As you practice using slow talk this week, see if you can feel the calmness in it, and be aware that when you use slow talk with other people, they will be more prone to listen to you because you sound calm.

Using slow talk will calm you down and reduce your anxiety.

Get started using slow talk:

- Practice slow talk by reading a handout over to yourself during your 30 minute a day study time. There are additional therapeutic handouts for you to read in the online session #2 materials.

- Each day, read over a handout to yourself, out loud, in slow talk. It may feel unusual at first, but that's because you're not used to reading clearly and precisely. Talk so that, if others were present, they could understand you. Don't rush your reading or speed up your speech.

- Practice using slow talk so that it becomes an automatic way of speaking, especially when you feel anxious. When you're anxious, deliberately refusing to speed up will control the level of adrenaline and cortisol in your system.

- Remember that slow talk is not a strange or mysterious process. All you're doing is *not* allowing anxiety to speed you up when you feel anxious.

Slow Thinking
Slowing our Automatic Racy Thinking Down

If we can slow our speaking down to stop the adrenaline and cortisol rush, then we can also learn to stop our racy, automatic negative thinking. If you understand the rationale behind slow talk and the physiological benefits it provides, let's bring this strategy over to our thinking habits, (i.e., our thought patterns).

Deliberately slowing down your thinking is something you can practice on and do. There is no self-consciousness involved in this process, so catch any fast, racy, automatic negative thinking – and deliberately slow it down. Do this in any way that works for you.

1. Find a distraction and pay attention to it.

2. Read a handout in slow talk, out loud, to yourself – this helps slow your thinking down.

3. Focus on what you're typing, texting, or writing, and gently keep your thoughts focused on the task at hand. If they wander, calmly bring them back to what you were focused on. Catch racy, out-of-control thinking, and gently slow it down.

4. Relax, slow down, loosen your muscles, and remind yourself that it is not productive to have automatic negative thoughts. Therefore, gently slow your thinking down.

5. Release the excessive adrenaline and cortisol in your body by telling yourself to take it easy, relax and lighten up.

6. Say to yourself: I don't need this pressure and stress.

7. I don't need this tension.

8. I need to think rationally about my life and about what I'm doing right now. I am not in a runaway car that's heading off the cliff. I am in control of my thoughts and actions.

9. My runaway thoughts are not in control of me. Ultimately, I am in control of my thoughts. With practice, I can slow my thinking down any time I choose to.

10. I have control over all these things. I choose to slow my thinking down, so that I can relax, think rationally, and feel calm.

11. I will put this strategy into place right now instead of procrastinating. I will think calmly whenever anxiety tries to scare and speed me up.

12. I will get more accomplished if I calm my thoughts down, so that my brain is clearer and better "organized." By taking my time – and not rushing – I will feel calmer and will be able to accomplish the things I need to do today.

Catch, Label, and Tell Your Brain the Truth

1. **Notice when you are having automatic negative thoughts or feelings.**

The first step in learning to think and believe rationally is to catch your old automatic negative thinking (ANTs). Note: When we say Automatic Negative Thinking, we also mean Automatic Negative Feelings, too. (For our purposes, ANTs are the same thing as ANFs).

2. **Stop this automatic negative thinking.**

Say "Stop!" or use the "Wait a minute!" statement:

"Hey, wait a minute! Stop! I'm having thoughts again that are not rational; thoughts that are not <u>healthy</u> or <u>helpful</u> to me."

Or use a visual method, such as seeing a red stop sign.

You have caught yourself thinking irrationally, so you *stop* the thought by saying "Wait a minute! Hold On! These thoughts are wrong" to yourself, and then...

Recognize ANTs as being toxic to your brain

3. **Find a distraction that can temporarily keep your brain away from ANTs.**

Just getting up, walking around, and reminding your brain that you are not going to give in to these thoughts and feelings anymore is a useful distraction.

See the "Distraction Suggestions" handout in your book for more ideas and suggestions about using distractions to keep your brain away from automatic negative thoughts.

A distraction should be something powerful for you, so that it will get your mind *away* from automatic negative thinking and onto something else. I've had people tell me that TV or the computer helps distract them, and, if it does, great.

But my thoughts were sometimes so negative that these distractions would not have been strong enough to help me.

I needed to get more active and move around in some way to get my mind completely away from automatic negative thinking, and then I had to find something really interesting or engrossing to keep my mind focused in a constructive direction and away from ANTs thoughts.

You need to find something that is strong enough for you to keep your mind on the distraction and away from your automatic negative thinking. Do not fight or battle with ANTs, and do not get angry over them. We must use our positive emotions to control and reduce our negative emotions. Getting your mind away from automatic negative thoughts is the right thing to do.

4. **Tell your brain the truth.** The brain doesn't automatically know what is good for you and what is harmful for you. If it did, you never would have developed social anxiety in the first place. The brain itself is "neutral." You have to tell it that you do not like these automatic negative thoughts and beliefs, and that you want to think rationally instead.

Again, from a calm perspective, you label these ANTs as "irrational," or "liars," or any other word that makes sense to you. You are labeling those thoughts, beliefs, and feelings as being harmful. You are telling your brain that you don't want to have these thoughts pop up automatically in your brain for the rest of your life.

Labeling these thoughts for what they are (irrational, ANTs, liars, bullies, etc.) keeps your brain aware of what you want to happen.

The stopping statement you make to your brain is rational. You are making a statement that your brain can comprehend, accept, and act on.

We never make ridiculous statements like, "When I wake up in the morning, I'll be the happiest person in the whole wide world." If you make a statement like that, good luck! It's too big, it can't be measured, and your brain won't believe it anyway. The main problem is that it's not a *rational* statement. When you wake up in the morning, you'll be the same old you.

We must stay realistic and rational in changing our thoughts.
Every therapy method we use will be rational and make common sense.
Because they are rational statements, your brain will accept them, believe them, and begin to act on them.

Distraction Suggestions

1. Exercising
2. Listening to music
3. Reading a good book
4. Swimming
5. Gardening
6. Surfing the internet
7. Talking to a positive friend
8. Watching a video tape – something funny
9. Walking around the block
10. Playing with or walking your pets
11. Going for a ride in the car
12. Sit down, de-stress, and slow talk to yourself
13. An interest or hobby you enjoy
14. Singing or humming along to music

A distraction can be ANYTHING that works for you – to temporarily get your mind off automatic negative thoughts (ANTs).

We need to stop our old thinking – block it off – as we learn to slowly develop new thinking habits (this is coming up…)

If we stop using the *old* anxiety neural pathways in our brain, then they eventually are *overwritten by neural pathways consisting of rational information.*

STOP that old, automatic negative thinking any way you can because it is poison…

Find as many distractions as you can to help you with your automatic negative thought stoppage.

Remember, there is a *physiological reason* that singing along to a favorite song or humming a tune under your breath is an effective distraction strategy for everyone.

The human brain uses a different area of the cerebral cortex to process singing than it does to process expressive and receptive speech. If your brain is using *more* of its energy to **sing** or hum, then it has *less* energy to use thinking automatic negative thoughts.

If you **exercise** for 20-30 minutes a day, you are flooding your body with endorphins, the body's natural "feel good" neurotransmitter. Exercising – in any way that works for you – is one of the best distractions, and has positive health benefits, too.

The ANTs Handout
Read this over to yourself, out loud, using slow talk every day

If the thoughts in your mind are intrusive, pressuring, anxiety-causing, negative, scary, obsessive, or irrational...

You are paying attention to <u>a</u>utomatic <u>n</u>egative <u>t</u>houghts (ANTs).

This is the same <u>a</u>utomatic <u>n</u>egative <u>t</u>hinking you've lived with for so long and has become a habit in your life.

Here is the truth:

The ANTS thoughts are always wrong. They always lie. They can never tell the truth.

Throw ANTs in the trash

The ANTS thoughts have no authentic power over me. That's why they're so scared I won't believe them. Their only hope is that I'll listen to them, believe them, and give them my power and attention. They feed and fuel themselves on my own old negative beliefs. If I don't accept and believe these old ANTs fears, they have no choice but to go away.

The ANTS voice is magnified by my anxiety, fear, and depression. To keep me feeling this way, the ANTS voice exaggerates, catastrophizes, puts me down, makes me feel guilty, robs me of my self-esteem, and makes my future look hopeless. These are all untrue – they are all lies – and it's about time I stopped believing them.

I must never listen to the lying ANTS voice. I know better. They always lead me in the wrong direction. They are a voice of negativism and defeat. They want to pull me down in the mud with them. I am not going to let them do this.

Even worse, The ANTS thoughts are *bullies*: they have no real power to use against me. They try to build on my own old feelings of depression, helplessness, and anxiety to pull me down.

If I catch on to what the ANTS are doing, and the lying ANTS thoughts feel like they are losing, then they try to put on more pressure. They tell me that anxiety, fear, embarrassment, catastrophe, and humiliation loom around every corner.

Thinking about making a public presentation or talking to an authority figure brings on stark, gut-wrenching fear. The ANTS love this one! I can almost see them dancing in glee!

The ANTs thoughts love my anxiety and fear! Because if I believe them, they have me trapped, entombed, and immobile. If I believe all these ANTS lies, I'll be stuck forever in my anxiety and depression. I'll never get any better. And all because I'm believing false, inaccurate, irrational lies from the past.

I must never listen to the lying ANTs voice.

The ANTs thoughts would love to prevent me from getting any better. All bullies like to see this happen to their victims.

But I don't have to listen and believe those ANTS thoughts. I do not choose to be a victim. I can see what they're trying to do to me now.

What can I do? I can say,

"Oh, it's that lying ANTs thought again. It's trying to frighten and depress me. It's telling me the same old lies. I refuse to believe them anymore. I've got better things to do than listen to a bullying liar."

I won't argue or fight against the ANTS thoughts. I've noticed that arguing comes from the negative emotions, and negative emotions never help me get better. The ANTS are good at arguing anyway... they love the pain and misery they cause me.

So, I'm going to do what they hate the most: I am not going to pay any more attention to them. I'll get up, get active, and do something else instead. I won't pay attention to those lying ANTs beliefs again.

Instead, I choose to calm down and ignore these lying automatic negative thoughts. These lying ANTS thoughts can't keep on talking forever. If I don't pay attention to them, they have to shrink and shrink and shrink and shrink…

What the ANTS hate worst of all is when I ignore them! They hate it when I won't listen to them and fall meekly into place like I used to do. Now I know better. I won't give in to the lying ANTs voice anymore.

Since they are pathological liars, and since their enjoyment comes from making me miserable, they don't like to give up. They may try a few new ways to throw a roadblock in my path, to scare me, or to confuse me about my progress. This is simply the ANTS way of trying to hold on to me and to keep me as one of its disciples.

Instead, I'll say to the ANTs:

"Oh, it's you again. You can't fool me anymore. I know this is just another one of your tricks to try and increase my anxiety. Well, you can try all you want. I don't care. I'm not going to listen to these lying ANTs thoughts again."

And then, I'll move on and use the strategies and distractions, read over this handout in slow talk, and I won't let them upset me anymore. I know that if I let them upset me, I am giving them my strength and power. If I don't let them upset me, and realize they don't have any power of their own, they have to shrivel up into nothing and go away for good.

The ANTS voice cannot tell the truth.

The ANTS voice is a loud and nasty bully: all gruff, bluff and no power.

The ANTS voice is only there to scare me. I won't let it happen anymore.

The ANTS voice exaggerates everything that is negative. It lies to me.

The ANTS voice has no real power over me – unless I decide to believe it.

The ANTS voice constantly lies, and liars are loud and like to be heard.

The ANTS hate it when I ignore them and say,

"SO WHAT?"

"Who cares?"

"Those ANTS thoughts couldn't tell the truth even if they tried..."

"Now, I can see that the ANTs thoughts are always wrong; they always lie – they can never tell the truth."

"I won't believe them anymore because, if I do, I'll be **trapped, entombed, and immobile.** I won't let that happen to me."

THE ANNUAL ANTS CONVENTION

Overheard at the ANNUAL ANTs CONVENTION...

Once a year, the ANTS from all around the world gather to visit each other and to show off how much they have grown. They're proud that they've grown *bigger* and *bolder* during the past year.

The Annual ANTS Conventions are like sales meetings, whereby the ANT that has made the most "sales" or "commissions" by increasing peoples' <u>A</u>utomatic <u>N</u>egative <u>T</u>houghts receives recognition, is greatly honored and highly praised.

The ANTS whole mission and goal in life is to fuel the negative thinking that leads to anxiety, in all its forms, and the related depression that goes along with it.

So, at the convention, the ANTS discuss new methods and strategies to rip us down, tear our self-esteem to shreds, and make us feel completely *hopeless* and *helpless* about our anxiety.

The ANT that comes up with the trickiest and most cunning plot to do this is always given a "special reward" and allowed to plague the people who have fully given in to ANTS thoughts, so that their lives are ruined and totally filled with fear and anxiety. They are kept on a very short and tight leash by the older and wiser ANTs.

Let's listen to some of this year's convention conversations:

Young ANT #1: "Hey, I've got another person convinced that he's no good, that he's not as important as other people, doesn't think he has any control over his own life. I've even got him scared to go out in public!"

Young ANT #2: "Ha! Another one of our victims trapped? I love it! (Clapping with glee.) What shall we give him? Panic attacks? Social anxiety? Obsessive-compulsive thoughts and behavior? Agoraphobia? (A special gleam appears in the ANTS' eye: "Or maybe all of the above."

Young ANT #1: "As long as he keeps believing us, we can give him as many problems as he'll take. Two problems are better than one, I always say..."

Young ANT #2: "Oh, man! I'm excited now! Maybe I'll win that award next year! I need to keep practicing my negative and irrational thinking and learn how to pass it on to others. Practice makes perfect, they always say..."

Young ANT #1: (snorting in pleasure): "But our victims never learn that practicing is important to change thoughts, do they? They start out practicing and being persistent, but they always quit before they really get any better. Then, we've got them trapped. One more defeat makes them feel totally worthless and helpless and then they really give up! Some of them give up right before they were going to get better. I love it when this happens."

The young ANTS continue to chortle in evil glee.

Just then, an older and wiser ANT enters the picture and overhears the conversation between the two young, immature ANTS.

Older and Wiser ANT Voice #3: "Stop your incessant bragging. You sound just like children! Don't you know that we derive our very existence from the lies we tell people that they believe? Every time you push too far there's a chance they'll get wise, and then we'll lose control. If the person ever fully realizes what we're doing to him, we're the ones who aren't going to have any power left..."

The younger ANTS shudder in horror at this statement.

Young ANT #1: (slowly and meekly) "You mean like our friend, the Destroyer? When that woman he was working on got some help and realized what was happening to her, she practiced and practiced and practiced..." (Young ANT #1 shudders violently at the thought).

Young ANT #2: (hesitatingly) "But what happened? What did this woman do anyway? And where is the Destroyer now?"

Older and Wiser ANT #3: "She realized what we were doing to her, caught onto him, and used peaceful, calming strategies to strip him of his power! And she wouldn't give up! No matter how many times we tried to trip her up, she just kept moving forward. Then she started using "slow talk" and reading "The ANTs Handout" and she actually practiced these abominations until they sank deeply down into her brain and became believable and automatic for her!"

Older and Wiser ANT #3 begins perspiring, his heart beats faster, and he starts getting dizzy, "Oh, my God! I don't think I can go on..."

Eventually, the lightheadedness and confusion cleared, he pulled himself together and spoke in a very low shaky voice: "The Destroyer began to get smaller and smaller, and the more he tried to bring back the anxiety, the fear, and the worry, the worse he became. She stood her ground, ignored him, and turned the other direction.

She refused to pay any attention to him. She started making friends and was no longer afraid to meet new people and do things with them. Finally, he had no energy left, he was sickly and frail, and he had to leave her brain. He ended up on the old insect farm for ruined and defeated ANTS: exhausted, permanently fatigued, and so very tiny and weak that he'll never leave the institution. He will continue to shrink and shrink and shrink until he dies. That nasty, vicious anxiety woman killed the Destroyer just by changing her thinking habits, and refusing to listen to him anymore."

Older and wiser ANT #3 looks around from immature ANT #1 to ANT #2, ruefully shaking his head... "Are you two learning anything from all this?"

Young ANT #1: (Scared, weak, trembling, and much more sober now): "You mean, we have to be careful not to get caught? If our person realizes what we're up to and stops believing in what we tell them, then... we're... we're..."

Older and Wiser ANT #3: "...DOOMED!

You'll spend the rest of your days on the dying ANTS farm with the Destroyer, feeling more and more miserable all the time, and continuing to shrivel up and shrink away. The good news is that you won't have to put up with the institution for very long. You'll grow so sickly, so tiny, so small and insignificant that you'll eventually just fade away into absolute nothingness.

And no one will ever remember that you even existed."

RATIONAL COPING STATEMENTS

The purpose of the rational coping statements for anxiety is to stop anxiety, and do it by reinforcing something rational. When these self-statements are practiced and learned, your brain takes over *automatically*. This is a form of "conditioning," meaning that your brain chemistry (its neurotransmission) actually changes as a result of your new thinking habits.

Pick only two or three statements, from the list that follows, that *you* like.

Pick the statements that make most sense and will help you stay rational, and repeat them to yourself out loud each day. You don't have to believe them fully yet – that will happen later.

Statements to use when Anxiety is Near:

1. I'm going to be all right. My feelings are not always rational. I'm just going to relax, calm down, and everything will be OK.

2. Anxiety is not dangerous – it's just uncomfortable. I am fine; I'll just continue with what I'm doing, or find something more active to do.

3. Right now, I have some anxious feelings I don't like. They are really just caused by adrenaline, however, and I can slow them down by calming myself. I will be fine.

4. I've stopped my negative thoughts before and I'm going to do it again now. I am becoming better and better at deflecting these ANTs and that makes me happy.

5. So I feel a little anxiety now, so what? It's not like it's the first time. I am going to take some nice deep breaths and keep on going. This will help me continue to get better.

Statements to use when Preparing for a Stressful Situation:

1. I've done this before so I know I can do it again.

2. When this is over, I'll be glad that I did it.

3. The feeling I have about this event doesn't make much sense. This anxiety is like a mirage in the desert. I'll just continue to "walk" forward until I pass right through it.

4. This may seem hard now, but it will become easier and easier over time.

5. I think I have more control over these thoughts and feelings than I once imagined. I am very gently going to turn away from my old feelings and move in a new, more rational direction.

Statements to use when I Feel Overwhelmed:

1. I can be anxious and still focus on the task at hand. As I focus on the task, my anxiety will go down.

2. Anxiety is an old habit pattern that my body responds to. I am going to calmly and nicely change this old habit. I feel a little bit of peace despite my anxiety, and this peace is going to grow and grow. As my peace and security grow, then anxiety will have no choice but to shrink.

3. At first, anxiety was powerful and scary, but as time goes by, it doesn't have the hold on me that I once thought it had. I am moving forward gently and nicely.

4. I don't need to fight my feelings. I realize that these feelings won't be allowed to stay around very much longer. I just accept my new feelings of peace, contentment, and calmness.

5. All these things that are happening to me seem overwhelming. But I've caught myself this time and I refuse to focus on these things. Instead, I'm going to talk slowly to myself, focus away from my problem, and continue with what I have to do. In this way, my anxiety will have to shrink up and disappear.

Neurophysiology: Brain Science, Neural Pathways and Associations
Neurons that Fire Together... Wire Together

In your brain, you have *hundreds of billions* of nerve cells (neurons) that are arranged in pathways, or networks (neural nets), much like the major interstates, freeways, and highways of a country.

Inside each of these neurons there is electrical activity, and between each neuron there is a small gap – in which chemicals, called neurotransmitters, are released.

You may have heard of some of the common neurochemicals in the synaptic gap: dopamine, serotonin, norepinephrine, GABA, and endorphins, among many others.

When your neurons fire together repeatedly, then they wire together, too.

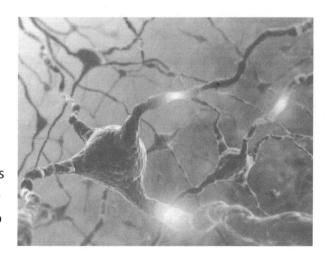

That is, when an event, such as talking to an authority figure, causes you to feel anxious, then the brain puts two and two together and realizes that every time you talk to an authority figure you feel anxious and scared. If the neurons fire together – (i.e., talking to an authority figure leads to fear) – then the brain circuits wire together.

If they fire together repeatedly, then the association in the brain becomes stronger. Thus, every time you think of talking to an authority figure, it causes anxiety.

Let's say you have anxiety about standing in front of people and making a presentation.

Your emotions about making a presentation (fear, anxiety, and worry) set off a flurry of activity in the brain: all of these neurons fire together at the thought of making a presentation.

The more that there is a flurry of firing together, the tighter and stronger the neurons wire together.

When you get anxious, your brain says,

"Danger! Help! I don't like this!"

So, this event – making a presentation – becomes associated with feelings of fear. When you know a presentation is coming up, boom! Almost instantaneously, you feel anxious and fearful.

The neurons in your neural pathways *fire* and *wire* together.

These two things become closely associated in the brain, so that thinking of making a presentation immediately brings up the feeling of anxiety.

Thankfully, the brain is very malleable, or "plastic," and can be changed.

You have an important part to play in this situation, because you are ultimately in control of changing your brain's neural pathways.

To get better, you must "interfere" and "interrupt" this firing and wiring of the brain's neural pathways.

What does this mean?

When we interfere with this association long enough, our neurons literally begin to form new pathways through our brains. Interfering means that you respond differently to presentations, so that the thought of giving a presentation no longer automatically brings up anxiety and fear. When you interfere with this association enough times, the neurons no longer fire and wire together.

When you begin responding differently to making presentations, then your brain gradually "re-organizes" the layout of your neural networks.

You have learned a new strategy or method to help you feel less anxious in this situation, and, as a result, you begin interfering with that old fire-and-wire connection.

Gradually, you no longer respond to the thought of making a presentation with high amounts of anxiety. You have permanently interfered with this association and your brain's neural pathway system changes as a result.

Social anxiety is a brain issue, and can be changed by using appropriate therapy that is specific to social anxiety disorder. That is exactly what you're doing in this series.

Note that you are interfering with anxiety's fire-and-wire connections every time you use a cognitive strategy against anxiety.

For example, using slow talk gradually calms you down and reduces anxiety. So when you think of mingling with other people, you remember you can use slow talk, instead of having immediate feelings of anticipatory anxiety. You are interfering and interrupting the old fire-wire connections.

Interfere and interrupt with the old wire-and-fire connections in any way possible. We've already learned several ways to do this – and we'll continue to learn more.

The JOYS of BEATING MYSELF UP

"After all, I've been beating myself up for so many years, it must be fun, right?"

This is what happens when I beat myself up:

1. I get to feel depressed, anxious, and worthless all at the same time. *THREE* emotions for the price of one! Very economical.

When I beat myself up:

2. I pay attention to and focus on events and situations that no one else thought were very important. By deliberately noticing all the little "mistakes" I make, I create my own "hell" all around me and get a chance to live in my own little world of pain and misery.

When I beat myself up:

3. I'm listening to ANTs thoughts, and I've found them to be very "truthful" and "accurate." By continuing to beat myself up, I am guaranteeing that my ANTs thoughts and feelings will always rule my life. They are such dear friends of mine.

When I beat myself up:

4. I reinforce the absolute fact that I am a failure, a loser, no good, and have nothing to offer anyone at any time. This fuels my anxiety and my darkest depression. It will mess up my life for good, and ensure that I do not have a future.

When I beat myself up:

5. I know I will continue to see things in the way the ANTs want me to see them... inaccurately, irrationally, and skewed to the negative. This is exciting! Maybe I can be known as the "most depressing person on the face of the planet" if I keep this up. I think I'll call the Guinness Book of World Records and find out. I deserve this award!

When I beat myself up:

6. I will not be allowing rational, accurate, and healthy thoughts to enter my mind. By beating myself up, I keep these nasty rational thoughts away forever. I am learning to *love* my anxiety, depression, fear, worthlessness, hopelessness, and failure.

WOW! Thank goodness for irrationality and untruths!
Now, I'm energized and ready to meet the day!
What are some other ways I can beat myself up and tear myself down? ☺

(Make sure you understand this is satire. It never helps to beat yourself up!)

ATTITUDES

Attitudes come from strongly-held beliefs, and beliefs are extremely powerful. Beliefs are saturated with emotion. That is, beliefs may be so strong, so powerful, and so emotionally charged, that, despite what is rational, they become the truth for the person believing them.

> *Beliefs are saturated with emotion*

Those of us with anxiety usually have many, many beliefs that are not true. We usually say they are irrational. But, let's be more honest about these irrational beliefs of ours:

Not only are they not true,
They are liars.
They are beliefs that are wrong. Therefore, these thoughts are liars.
If we continue to believe these irrational lies, we will be stuck in our anxieties forever.

Here are some "I" statements that will help you believe what is rational as you are say them out loud to yourself (i.e., to your brain):

Healthy, Rational "I" statements

- "I choose to move forward. I open my mind so that I can believe the truth."
- "I choose to be mentally healthy."
- "I choose to believe my rational thoughts."
- "I choose to believe the truth, instead of old, irrational, negative ANTs thoughts."

Your negative beliefs may be so strong that you can't see the light at the end of the tunnel. If so, this is perfectly normal. At first, it was very hard for me to believe anything rational about myself or the way I interacted with the world.

My thoughts had been negative for so many years that they seemed permanent and intractable. Thankfully, they were not. The brain *is* malleable, it *does* change, and this is an example, as neuroscientists call it – of "brain plasticity."

Your beliefs, too, must move in the direction of becoming more truthful and rational. Many times we can question our negative beliefs through short statements that are already emotional in nature.

For example,

WHO CARES?

SO WHAT?

WHY AM I DWELLING ON THIS?

I'M TIRED OF MAKING A MOUNTAIN OUT OF A MOLEHILL!

I'VE GOT BETTER THINGS TO DO THAN WORRY ABOUT THIS!

IT'S NO BIG DEAL!

These attitudes carry emotional feelings along with them already. As deliberately as we can, let's take these attitudes and use them against social anxiety.

Some examples of how to use the "Attitude" Statements:

If someone doesn't like me, *who cares*? That's their problem! I am a fine person and they've totally misinterpreted who I am. It's their problem and it's their loss. If they're such a bad judge of character, I don't want to know them anyway!

So I didn't do a perfect job, *so what?* I did better than many other people do. I can only do my best anyway – I can't be perfect. Everyone can't be my friend, and I wouldn't *want* to be friends with everyone anyway. So who cares? So what?

I didn't do anything that strange or embarrassing!

The situation is over and done with. Time to move forward.

So, why am I dwelling on this? All I did was talk to someone for a few minutes. I don't need to pick apart every word I said, and replay the scene in my mind over and over again. Little things like this have happened many times in the past, and no one but me even remembers them.

I don't need to constantly rehash the past. So why am I dwelling on it? It's water under the bridge and it's ruining my life. Who cares anyway? So what!

Why do I care so much what other people think about me? I've got better things to do than worry about that! If they don't like me, too bad! Why should I care so much about other people's approval?

Rationally, it's my own approval that counts. I don't need to bow and scrape before everyone else and beg for their approval. Who cares? So what!

So, I've got problems in my life! Who doesn't? I'm tired of making a mountain out of a molehill. I don't need to make my problems bigger than they already are! It's no big deal! Everyone has problems and they make it through somehow. I can make it through, too, and there's no reason for me to get frustrated. I'm blowing things way out of proportion. It's just no big deal!

You have used all these attitude statements in your life already, in some way, in the past. Let's bring them in to the area of social anxiety.

If you have anticipatory anxiety over an upcoming event, so what? It's no big deal. The situation is not going to end your life!

It's better to find a distraction to deal with it, than give in to the negative thought cycle and constant worry. After all, why should I be dwelling on this garbage anyway? I've got better things to do than to listen to bullying liars.

If someone doesn't like what I've done, who cares? They can go take a flying leap. All I can do is the best I can. I can't do anything more than that. Worrying never did me any good. I'm tired of making a mountain out of a molehill! It's no big deal!

See if you can practice these simple attitude statements by themselves at first, just to get in the habit of remembering them, using the right tone of voice, and having them start to appear in your mind.

Notice your tone of voice as you say them and try to imitate me, if necessary. The tone of your voice sends a clear message to your brain.

When you say, "who cares?" or "it's no big deal," your brain not only gets the message, it interprets the emotional feeling as well. Your tone of voice is important because we are reaching the brain in the two ways that are necessary for progress.

Fairly soon, in a real life situation, these attitude statements are going to pop into your mind.

Then, take those thoughts, repeat them, and make the feeling even stronger. Each and every time you do that, the stronger and more powerful your new attitudes and emotions will become.

The "Look Around Technique"
How to Decrease Self-Consciousness

If it feels like people are watching you, judging you, or that you are on display, see whether this is really true by testing this out for yourself using the

"Look-Around Technique"

When you're out in public or when other people are around, if you start to feel self-conscious, like you are being monitored, assessed, judged, or evaluated, let's find out what's really happening. *Are* we being watched and judged? Or are we just imaging it? Or perhaps it's a little bit of both, but let's not just talk about it. Let's do something about it and find out the whole truth.

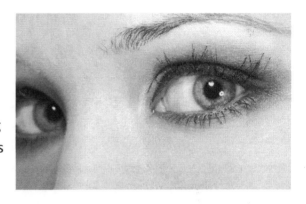

When you're out in public, don't add to your inhibitions and fears by keeping your eyes fixed in one direction, so that you can avoid other people's glances. Refusing to look around will always keep you inhibited, closed in, and fearing the worst.

Instead, slowly look around your environment to see how many people are actually staring back at you with judgment in their eyes. The only way for you to really believe the truth – to see what is really happening – is if you test this out for yourself.

Let's say you are walking through a crowded shopping mall and you begin to feel people are looking at you and judging you. You feel it's a negative judgment and you're under inspection. No one likes to feel this way, so it makes you very *self-conscious*.

Stop for a moment with me and let's rationally go over this. How likely is it that people everywhere in the mall are looking at you and judging you negatively? What are they judging you about? It must be something big for so many people –

independently of each other – to be focusing all their attention on you. You must be doing something drastically out of the ordinary to get this kind of reaction.

Or, is nothing really going on at all? Is most all of it in your head? Are you making this assessment because of your *feelings*? Do you really need to feel self-conscious and inhibited? Or could it be that it's just an old ANTs habit that got triggered by being in the shopping mall and around so many other people?

Rationally, is there any reason to feel self-conscious?

The only way you are going to get this answered to your own satisfaction is by testing this out for yourself. It doesn't make much difference what others tell you, because it's the way you feel about the situation that creates self-consciousness.

If you feel self-conscious and anxious, then these emotions have taken you away from being rational. Based on the way you feel, it's likely you believe that people are singling you out, judging you somehow, and evaluating you in a negative fashion. It almost feels like you are under a microscope and people are watching everything you do.

So to find out the truth – to find out what is rational in this situation – we need to test this idea out for ourselves. We need to prove to ourselves what is really going on.

Here's what to do when you're feeling self-conscious in public:

Slowly and gradually look around, just like everyone else does. You are not looking at other people in the eyes or trying to attract attention. You are just gently looking around to get an idea of what's going on around you.

If you have your eyes averted and are always looking at the ground, you will never know what is actually happening all around you. If you only look at the part of the mall where no one is at, you will not get the chance to see, with your own two eyes, what is really going on.

We can gently use the "Look Around Technique" right away – in any situation where we feel closed off, inhibited, and self-conscious.

Just try it calmly. It's not difficult to do, and it doesn't leave you feeling nervous and anxious. Instead, it makes you feel more comfortable and less anxious. You are more in control because you are *acting* on your environment, instead of merely *reacting* to it.

All that's involved in the look around technique is that you look around and see what's really going on. Feel free to relax your muscles as you do this, and let any tension go. Slow yourself down and look around the room gently.

If you are sitting down in a place where you feel self-conscious, don't tense your muscles up as a defense mechanism. Loosen yourself up and relax instead.

Move your body around so that you feel comfortable. If you're standing up, shift from one foot to the other, reach out for a magazine with your hand, scratch your face, or clear your throat.

Then, gently look around the room, and observe what is actually happening.

What you observe when you use the "Look Around Technique" may surprise you – and take away some of your feelings of self-consciousness. Your feelings of inhibition and inaction will go down as well.

Anytime you're feeling self-conscious, gently look around yourself and see whether people are judging you or not. Is there really any need to feel self-conscious?

Test it out, and prove it to yourself.

SETBACKS HAPPEN TO EVERYONE
Let's Turn Them Around and Make Progress

As you make progress against social anxiety, it's likely you will have a "setback" or two along the way. It happens to everyone – you can't have a setback unless you've made some progress first.

Progress in overcoming social anxiety never occurs in a straight "linear" fashion anyway. As we make progress, we find that there are mountains and valleys, and we need to understand that after we've taken three steps forward, something might surprise us and cause us to take one step back. This is normal at this stage, and is not something to worry over or beat yourself up about. Be nice to yourself instead.

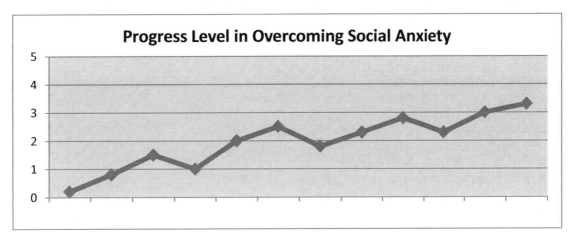

Everyone has setbacks because none of us are perfect. This is the way the human brain is constructed when learning new things. You are still making progress even after you've had a setback, and you learn a lot of rational information from every setback you have. However, because setbacks do not feel good, we're going to learn how to stop them.

What is the true test of whether you are making progress? Progress can be measured in many ways, but figuratively it can be seen as moving up three steps... and moving back one step. The "moving back" is a setback. But you can recover quickly and continue moving forward after a setback. So that, looked at over a week or a month, you are making steady progress forward. But one time in the week you may have been set back.

If anxiety surprises you, or you forget to use your anti-anxiety strategies, a temporary setback can occur. But this proves you are making progress. You can't have a setback if you haven't made progress first.

Setbacks are normal on the road to getting better – the brain is still processing everything you're learning and doing – and setbacks go away altogether as you take control away from anxiety and the old ANTs habits and beliefs.

Notice the diagram in this handout. It helps to visually look at what a setback is in terms of a graph or chart. As you can see, setbacks mean you are already making progress. It's not linear progress, though. Setbacks do occur. But over the long term, you are always moving forward and always making progress against social anxiety.

You are always getting better, because you are moving incrementally – one step at a time. But in the short term, you may have an upsetting experience that brings back anxiety. A setback is emotional, and may seem devastating when it happens. But it is merely an ANTs trick, and you lose none of the progress you've already made at all. It's the pull of negative emotions that try to keep you stuck in social anxiety.

The key element here is that you recognize the setback as a setback – *and nothing more*. It is a sign of progress, not of failure. You will soon see you haven't "lost" anything you've already learned. You haven't lost any of your knowledge, your cognitive strengths, or abilities. It's all there still. You learned it, it became part of your brain's neural pathway system, and it is permanent. It is not something you can lose.

What you need to do after an emotional setback, after anxiety surprised you, and you feel down and defeated, is get up, dust yourself off, spray those pathologically lying ANTS with insecticide, and keep moving on with your life.

Whatever therapy you have already learned is still there in your brain – regardless of how you feel. Negative feelings can temporarily cloud over your rationality, but the moment you get rational again, you'll see that everything you've learned in therapy is still there in your brain, ready to use.

You are making permanent progress by doing cognitive therapy. You cannot relapse from what you've already learned, just like you cannot un-teach a person how to speak their native language or un-teach them to drive a car. You may feel like everything is lost after a setback – but when you calm down and get rational, you can tell that everything you've learned is still there – it just needs additional reinforcement.

If the ANTs pull us down and trick us into negative emotions about our progress, they do it because negative emotions cloud over the rational thinking of our brain. The ANTs play around with your emotions to keep you dangling on their string. The ANTs don't want to see you get better and leave them.

They're accustomed to the familiarity of your neural pathway system and they feel comfortable with you. They know your weaknesses, and they'll use them whenever they can, until you start to understand what they're doing and put a stop to it.

After a setback, we often perversely feel like giving in to the ANTs and throwing a pity party for ourselves. It still feels natural, because our brain messages have traveled down this route for many years. But we're interrupting the old fire-and-wire connections in the brain – change is occurring, and a setback won't keep you down long. **The moment you get rational with yourself, you will feel better again.**

It sounds like an adolescent love song, but it's exasperatingly real.
When you get negative emotions under control, you will be able to feel and see things rationally. You haven't lost anything – everything you've learned and done already is still in the brain ready for you to use.

A setback cannot change anything you've already done or learned – that is, a setback cannot change the new neural pathways you're developing in the brain. You cannot relapse from what you've already learned and done.

As the days pass, you are getting more rational about all this. It's important that we continue to reinforce the rational therapy and the solutions to social anxiety into our brains. That is how we get better.

The nice – and always predictable – thing about this is if you continue forward – even after a setback – it isn't too long before things get a little easier for you – and you can see the reason for the setback. In the long run, there's always something you achieve and learn from a setback that makes your progress stronger and more permanent.

The old saying, "When you fall off the horse, get right back on again" applies here. If you recognize the setback as simply a setback, say to yourself:

> "It's those lying ANTS again, making me worry and doubt myself. They think they're going to win. They think I'm going to give up and throw in the towel. They expect to keep me afraid, scared, nerve-wracked, and anxious for the rest of my life.

> I have news for them: That setback just made things clearer to me, because I have no intention of listening to lying ANTs beliefs anymore. I understand what just happened. Now, I know how to stop it from happening again. I'm moving on with my life and reinforcing my therapy, despite anything that anxiety throws at me..."

When the road is tough and everything seems difficult, it helps to remember that anyone who is persistent and doesn't give up, always makes it over the top of the hill.

Setbacks happen to everyone. They are proof that you're making progress. Knowing all this will make it easier to catch and stop yourself from having another setback.

If you do have a setback, catch it, tell your brain "No way I'm giving in to anxiety and feeling sorry for myself," and then get up and get active right away. Exercise. Sing. Talk to a positive friend. Talk out loud to yourself, using a handout. Go grocery shopping. Do something active and positive.

You'll feel better in a short period of time and you'll see that you can still be calm and rational and in control of your life. **A setback is just the ANTs deceptive love call – they want you paying attention to them, and when you're not, they like to upset you as much as possible.**

But you're too smart for that now. You know what's really going on. A setback is unpleasant, but it's just a setback, and it's proof that you've got the ANTs on the run.

Setbacks are a normal part of this journey in overcoming social anxiety.

You are on the right track. Let's keep moving forward, using your anti-anxiety methods and strategies to overcome social anxiety.

A "Balance Sheet" for Facing Anxiety

ONE EXTREME
Avoidance
It Doesn't Work

ANOTHER EXTREME
Flooding
It Doesn't Work

Notice these two extremes. On the one side, completely avoiding activities and situations only makes us more fearful and anxious. The more we consistently avoid situations, the worse our social anxiety becomes.

On the other extreme, we see that flooding ourselves with highly anxiety-producing activities does not work either – instead, it reinforces our feelings of failure and inadequacy, and it makes us even more anxious than we already are.

The Solution to this Dilemma is To:

1. Start behavioral therapy slowly. We take one small step at a time because of the danger flooding causes. If anything causes too much anxiety, then don't do it at the present time, if possible.

2. Plan to do something that is only *slightly* anxiety producing – something that makes you a little nervous maybe, but something you know you can do and can assess rationally after it is over. Take one small step.

By doing what you planned to do, you are no longer avoiding. But you are also not flooding yourself with fear, because you are deliberately taking a small step, one that doesn't cause much anxiety. It is important to start behavioral therapy in this manner.

3. Loosen up, relax your muscles, slow down, take a deep breath.

4. Use a rational statement before you do a behavioral experiment. For example, say to yourself, "Saying hello to a stranger was something that used to cause me anxiety in the past. Things are a little easier now and I think that it may not be that big of a deal."

(Change the wording to fit your own personal circumstance.)

You are taking one step, meaning it doesn't cause you much anxiety. In some cases, it may cause no anxiety at all, and that is a good place to start, so that we have a guideline or a baseline to chart our steps.

5. Always err on the side of *caution*. Taking one small step is the right decision to make.

You are challenging and breaking up your old belief system when you talk to yourself and let the brain know you are going to take one small step against anxiety, with the understanding that you are making progress – this is forward movement. Approaching anxiety in this way keeps you on track.

6. When you are cognitively prepared, go ahead with your experiment, but start slowly – one step at a time – with an activity that only causes a small amount of anxiety.

7. Expect a little nervousness, but continue to stay rational. Slow yourself down and loosen your muscles. Use the strategies we've learned so far to lessen anxiety.

8. Focus on the *external* situation around you. What is someone saying to you? What is going on around you? Listen to other people and what they're saying.

Stay in the present moment – there is no need to focus internally on yourself. Focus outwardly on what is happening around you.

9. If you find the anxiety is too strong, you have taken more than one step... so feel free to leave the situation and think rationally about what just happened. The importance of thinking rationally – getting the emotional reasoning out of the picture – cannot be emphasized enough.

10. Congratulate yourself for carrying out this experiment. You are successful because you took that one step. We must learn to give ourselves credit, and not beat ourselves up, when we face an anxiety situation in the right way – one small step at a time – and work against anxiety.

11. The fact that you made the decision to do a behavioral experiment is a victory in and of itself. This is something you were not doing last week. You *are* doing it this week. That is a small step, but it is progress, and you did it. That's all that's important. This is a rational fact. You did what you needed to do and you survived.

12. When you feel ready, move up to a slightly more anxiety-producing situation. That is, take another step forward.

The Fighting Paradox

A paradox is something that opposes our normal way of thinking. It is something that seems impossible to solve. A paradox, by definition, is counterintuitive.

A paradox involves doing the opposite of what you think you should do in a situation. By doing the things we think we should do to get better – we end up making our social anxiety worse.

We actually get better by doing the opposite of what we expect or feel. The solution to social anxiety is counterintuitive. It is a paradox.

Let me explain:

Fighting my anxiety and fear seemed natural to me – so I did it. But every time I fought it, I ended up bloodied and defeated. I tried speaking in public, talking to small groups of adults, speaking to my bosses and supervisors, and I pushed myself and forced myself to do things that caused me anxiety, thinking that I was facing my fears and I would get better.

But forcing myself to do anxiety-causing things never made me feel better. Flooding myself with anxiety never helped me get a handle on anxiety. Why? Because I was using a negative emotion (aggression) to try to cure another negative emotion (anxiety).

Using a negative emotion to fight a negative emotion doesn't work.

Any time I used a negative emotion to try and make myself better – to try to overcome my social anxiety – my anxiety only became stronger and more persistent.

The things I did that I thought would help me – kept me trapped in my anxiety instead. Each time I tried and failed, I reinforced my anxiety and made it stronger. We call this concept "The Fighting Paradox."

These are the five negative behaviors I used on a regular basis to try to get over my social anxiety. These are the behaviors that don't work:

1. I **INSISTED** that I shouldn't feel anxious. Why should I be afraid of meeting other people or going to parties? Why should I be uncomfortable at restaurants and other public places? Why should I feel out of place and awkward? I *shouldn't*, I told myself – and I kept on insisting to myself that it just wasn't right!

2. I **FOUGHT** the feelings of fear and anxiety by using ANGER: "I'm going to get over this today, dammit! I'm sick and tired of living this kind of life. I want my life back. I want to feel happy and peaceful. I hate to feel weak, alone, and afraid!" Then, I would punch a pillow, kick a door, or slam something to the ground in anger. This didn't dissipate my anxiety. It only reinforced it.

> For every minute you are angry... you lose 60 seconds of happiness

Using anger as a means to overcome anxiety doesn't work.

3. I **BEMOANED** the fact that I had social anxiety. "Why must I have this stuff anyway? No one else has it. They can do whatever they want. I can't even make friends. They get good jobs and have families, but I have no one I can even talk to. And it'll never get any better... I'll always be alone – I'll always be miserable – I'll never have any friends! I'll be anxious, miserable, and fearful until the day I die!" I threw quite a few pity parties for myself over the years, but no matter how much I felt sorry for myself, it never made me any better. There was no value in feeling sorry for myself. It only caused me more pain and wasted valuable time.

4. I used the "**FAIRNESS**" Argument: "It's not fair that I have this! I didn't do anything wrong. It's not fair that I'm the only one in the whole world who has to suffer with these feelings of fear and despair!"

That is a rational statement, but what good does repeating it do? Even though it is true, it offers no solutions.

There is no solution in going around saying, "It's not fair." OK, you're right. It's not fair. So, did saying that make you better? In the long run all it does is reinforce your problems and make them bigger. You make no progress by continually saying "it isn't fair."

5. I used the "**DESERVING**" Argument: "This anxiety is so terrible. I don't *deserve* to go through this. I never did anything to deserve this. I've never hurt anyone. I'm a good person. What did I do to deserve this chronic, daily fear?"

This is the same thing as the excuse argument. It may be true that we don't deserve to have social anxiety, but there is no solution in going around and saying to yourself "I don't deserve this."

Fighting, battling, and struggling are all normal human reactions to dealing with the incredible emotional pain that social anxiety causes, and when you have a problem as severe as this, it is natural that you want to get rid of it in any way possible.

Unfortunately, using the lines of reasoning I used against anxiety is similar to throwing gasoline on a raging fire.

Resisting the anxiety, fighting the anxiety, battling the anxiety, attacking the anxiety, or getting aggressive with the anxiety – just brings the anxiety on stronger. This is why we call the solution to social anxiety a "paradox." The things we normally expect to do to get better, only end up making the problem worse.

For example, every time I aggressively tried to battle my anxiety, I threw myself into tough situations that were big anxiety causing events for me, and the end result was that I felt even more down and depressed.

I survived the anxiety-provoking situation, but the high levels of anxiety and fear I went through made me feel defeated and hopeless. I was reinforcing my existing anxiety. Why should I do that?

I saw myself as a failure and a loser, because I didn't get over my anxiety like I planned. Anxiety was still there, making my life miserable. Little did I know that I made my social anxiety worse by pressuring myself to move too far too fast!

I shouldn't have forced myself or pressured myself – because my aggression only fueled my anxiety and set it on fire. The struggling, battling, and pressuring only made my anxiety worse. Like a Chinese finger trap, the more I fought it, the tighter its hold on me grew.

To get better, we must use counterintuitive strategies. The solution to anxiety is a paradox. Look at it this way:

That which you resist... persists

Think about this saying for a minute, because it encapsulates the entire meaning of the anxiety paradox:

That which you resist, persists

If we resist anxiety, it will continue to persist and rule our lives. Resisting, fighting, and battling anxiety is not the answer to the problem... it IS the problem.

Anxiety loves it when you fight against it, wail against it, and agonize over it. When you fight against anxiety, you lose.

That which you resist, persists

Anxiety loves it when you feel hopeless and dejected. It has you trapped.

Anxiety loves it when you curse fate for making you socially anxious. It has you trapped.

Anxiety loves it when you get depressed and think you'll never get any better. It has you trapped.

Anxiety loves it when you verbalize defeat and say you can't see light at the end of the tunnel. It has you trapped.

Anxiety will only respond and begin to disappear when we approach it using our positive emotions – our calmness and our rationality.

Here's the way to overcome anxiety: **We meet anxiety-provoking situations as calmly as possible. We are not meeting it by resisting, fighting, battling, or struggling with it.**

Instead, we accept ourselves, calm ourselves down, loosen up our muscles, and take a nice deep breath.

We slow our thinking down and remember to use slow talk if we're in a social situation.

By staying in our positive emotions – and not using our old negative strategies to try to conquer anxiety – we continue to make progress against it.

As we do this, it makes it easier for us to realize what anxiety has been doing to us all these years. Now, armed with this new knowledge, we're going to learn how to respond to anxiety-provoking situations differently.

In the past, we responded to anxiety by involuntarily tensing up our muscles to prepare a defense against anxiety. This does not work.

We should not be tensing our muscles up. Instead, we should be doing the opposite. (This is a paradox, right?)

Say to yourself,

"I will loosen up and relax. I'll calm down as much as possible and take it easy on myself."

Since the solution to social anxiety is paradoxical, we need to do the opposite of what we've done in the past. No fighting, battling, or struggling. No more pity parties. No more "I don't deserve this!" arguments. The solution to social anxiety is counterintuitive and paradoxical. We're going to approach it in this manner.

Bears Attack & Maul, Bees Swarm & Sting
A follow-up to "The Fighting Paradox"

Finally, you've gotten away from it all, and you're on that camping trip you've been planning for months. You found just the right place to set up camp, dinner over the open fire was great, and as far as you can see, the sky is filled with beautiful shimmering stars. All of a sudden, out of nowhere, you hear a loud, rustling noise…

You look up to glimpse a grizzly bear entering your campsite. You do a double-take, because a grizzly bear is the last thing you expect to see. But there it is.

Now, any sane person would be afraid. The adrenaline would immediately start pumping throughout your body, your thoughts would begin to race, and undoubtedly you would be sweating.

But what is the safest thing to do?

The adrenaline tells you to run, escape, get out of there, move as quickly as you can toward safety.

But another voice inside you is more rational. It says, "Hold on. Slow down. Wait a minute. If I run, if I try to escape, if I move too quickly, I will be attracting the grizzly bear's attention. Since I don't want to aggravate the situation, I think it might be better if I stand perfectly still."

If you listen to your first voice and turn and run away in fear, the bear will likely run after you… and he won't be in a friendly mood.

Instead of running, escaping, avoiding, and fleeing out of fear,

Have you ever played dead?

Do you see the analogy? When anxiety comes to attack us, drag us down, create panic, intensify our worst social fears, speed up our racy and obsessional thinking... these feelings should serve as a red flag.

If a bear enters your life, the worst possible thing you can do is run. The bear will catch you, claw you, maul you... and *you* will be the worse for it. If you stand your ground and don't run, the bear is likely to leave you alone.

By the same token, if a swarm of bees is buzzing around your head, the *worst* possible thing you can do is to make the bees mad. If you panic, throw your arms into the air, and flail them around, the bees will zero in on you, fly right on to your skin, and sting you mercilessly.

So, what do you do when anxiety tries to attack and hurt you?

Play dead. Do not respond. Do not panic. Slow down. Take your time. Use your rational statements.

Say to yourself: "If I stay calm, then anxiety will not be able to sting me..."

You already know the more you fight, battle, struggle, and attack, the more the bear will maul – and the more the bee will sting.

You have *control* over the bear and the bee. Use the fighting paradox to take anxiety down another peg. Calm down, relax, cool it, move to the peace zone. Do not respond to negativity by using a negative emotion.

Anxiety likes it when you fight back because then it has you trapped. The bear and the bee will claw and sting you if you fight them back. On the other hand, if you are calm and still, they will ignore you... you are not giving them any power to be able to harm you.

Don't get stung by the anxiety bee or mauled by the anxiety bear. Take it easy, slow talk, stay calm... then they will continue to have less and less power over you... and you will realize that you are the one who is in charge.

Don't Feed and Fuel Anxiety:
Let it Starve and Disappear

Social anxiety has no authentic, genuine power to use against you.

It uses its own old power, your own old thoughts, and the way you were mentally conditioned when you were younger – to keep you stuck, trapped in the vicious circle, and feeling hopeless and helpless about ever getting out.

If you believe what anxiety tells you, just as Dorothy believed the wicked witch, then anxiety has you trapped, entombed, and immobile.

You must never listen to the lying witches' voice. But the wicked witch had no real authentic power – just as social anxiety is built on a foundation of **irrationality** and **lies**.

Here are some rational statements you can use to sink the lessons of the "Fighting Paradox" into your brain:

- "I will not give anxiety my strength and power."

- "I will respond to anxiety with calmness and peace."

- "I will use my 'who cares' and 'so what?' attitude when anxiety comes calling."

- "Anxiety has no power of its own. I am the one who fuels it and gives it its strength and power. I am no longer going to do this."

- "I'm tired of letting anxiety rule my life. It will not let it scare me any longer."

- "I will no longer feed and fuel my anxiety and fear. Maybe my anxiety, and my focus on it, has kept me feeling anxious all these years."

- "I no longer will feed my anxiety and fear. Instead, I will relax, take it easy, and realize the situation may be easier than it seems."

- "Anxiety can only rule if I am scared and am afraid. I decide to calm myself down as much as I can, relax and loosen my muscles, and focus on calmness and peace instead."

- "My choice is to react to anxiety with calmness."

- "I have been fooled by anxiety for too long. Anxiety causes more anxiety because I have given it all my emotional power in the past. I have believed it. Now I know that it is not true, and that my own fear made my fear stronger."

- "I will stay away from the vicious cycle of anxiety. Fear causes fear which causes more fear. I am tired of giving in to fear. I have decided to approach life with as much calmness and peace as possible."

- "The ANTs thoughts are always wrong. They can never tell the truth. They always lie."

Einstein's Definition of "Insanity"

"Insanity = doing the same thing over and over again, but expecting a different result."

Stop and think about this for a moment. If you want to achieve something, you do something to accomplish your goals. But what if what you do doesn't work, and doesn't allow you to achieve what you want to achieve? What do you do?

Humans, and this is particularly applicable to those of us with social anxiety, have a tendency to keep doing the same things over and over again, even when we know they don't work. Of course, this is irrational and illogical, but we still do it.

SAME ACTIONS = SAME RESULTS

When it comes to anxiety, we automatically respond to it in the same way that we did ten years ago, or ten months ago. Whatever we're doing didn't work then, and it doesn't work now. We feel anxiety, and are in the habit of responding to it in the same way every time. Unfortunately, we also get the same results.

It is irrational to expect a different result if we keep doing the same things. For those of us with social anxiety, this quote has great relevancy. There is a big lesson for us to learn. Let's look at it in more detail.

In the past, we tended to do the same things over and over again and hoped that our anxiety would go away somehow. That's only human nature.

Although what we've done to get over social anxiety has never worked, we still respond to anxiety in the same way we've been responding for years. They become entrenched brain habits because we use them over and over again. Our old ways of dealing with anxiety include trying to avoid it, stressing ourselves out with anticipatory anxiety, and trying to tame it aggressively.

We keep responding to anxiety in the same ineffective ways, even though they have never worked for us in the past. As a result, anxiety has continued to terrorize our lives for many years. To keep responding to it in the same way, habitually, year in and year out, is irrational, illogical, and a little bit insane.

We need to be aware that we can approach and respond to anxiety-provoking events in a different way – in a new way – that will bring us results. That is, by doing something different, we can really see our anxiety lessening its grip on our lives.

In the past, we acted illogically. But now we know better, and we know what to do to get better. Einstein's definition of insanity is a continual reminder that we're learning new methods and strategies that work to help us overcome social anxiety.

We can't keep doing the same things over and over again if they aren't working. We need to change course and do something different. By realizing that the solution to anxiety is a paradox, (doing the opposite of what we've been doing) we'll begin to use new and different strategies to deal with our problem.

Loosen Up and Let Stress Go

When you are feeling anxious, because of anticipatory anxiety, worry, or ANTs thoughts of any kind...

Just remember these two words... "Loosen Up"
If you're in public or in a social situation and you're feeling anxious,
Just remember these two words... "Loosen Up"

What happens when we're anxious is that the muscles in our body tighten up – so that we can be prepared for the "danger" facing us. This happens automatically, many times without us realizing it.

Technically, our physical body is preparing to meet a threatening challenge that really isn't there – but, since we think it is, our muscles become tight and rigid anyway.

I first noticed this one Saturday morning over thirty years ago when I was driving down the freeway to the library. The library was a safe place for me to go because it was fifteen miles from home and I knew I wouldn't run into anyone that I knew there.

But as I drove down the freeway, I glanced down at my hands and saw they were chalk white from gripping the steering wheel so tightly. I was holding on to the steering wheel for dear life with both hands! It surprised me that I was that tense and stiff. After thinking about it, I figured out why I went into "automatic" stress mode and gripped the steering wheel so tightly:

#1 – I was terribly self-conscious. Even though only a few cars drove past me, I still felt as if the nameless people in the nameless cars were staring at me as they passed me by. I kept my eyes straight ahead and avoided the situation, so as to avoid the gazes I felt I would get if I looked over at the passing cars.

#2 – I had been tensing my muscles up for so many years that it had become a routine habit for me. Tightening up my muscles was an ingrained habit of mine.

As time went by, I began to notice that I tensed up quite a lot in any social situation. So, gradually, I began to catch myself tensing up.

When I noticed this, I took a deep breath, and deliberately let go of the tension to let me "loosen up" a little. This helped me out a great deal.

But I didn't know enough then to be systematic about it. I did not practice the solution to this at all. I didn't stay consistent in doing what I needed to do to change my brain and reduce my anxiety.

By realizing this and just letting go of the tension in your muscles – by "loosening up" – you are calming yourself down and making the situation a little easier for yourself.

The other positive element is that as you let go and let your muscles become loose, limp, and relaxed, you are reminding and reinforcing your brain that the stress and anxiety you're experiencing is just an old, useless, ANTS habit.

Let that tightness in your muscles go – loosen up, let it go, release it – quiet your body down – It's time we started believing the truth about ourselves instead of old, irrational ANTS lies.

The truth is that there is nothing to fear, we can handle situations fine, and we can do a much better job at coping than we ever imagined.

Let's respond to anxiety by calming down, slowing down, and loosening our muscles up. Try this out for yourself. You'll feel a little less stressed out from the beginning.

As with all the new strategies, it is important that you start this "loosening up" process at home, when you are alone. You should practice it at home first, when you are not feeling anxiety, so that it can enter your brain when you are facing anxiety.

If you try this strategy for the first time in a public, highly-anxious situation, it may not work for you and you will feel defeated before you ever begin. Please start the process out slowly, at home, when you're alone and feeling OK.

Practice on it until you feel more calm, relaxed, and less stressed.

Then, we will respond to anxiety situations in real life in a brand new way: We will take it easy, slow ourselves down, loosen our muscles, relax, and take a deep breath.

- When I start to feel anxiety, I will relax and loosen up my muscles instead of tensing up

- I will loosen up, relax my muscles, and let stress go

- I will take a deep breath, relax, and feel the calmness and peace grow

- I will stop resisting anxiety and relax and loosen up instead

- As I relax and loosen up, my anxiety goes down

- Be persistent, not resistant. I persistently relax and calm down. There is no external enemy to fight

- I react to anxiety with as much calmness as possible

How to Temporarily Cut Down on Feelings of Anxiety

This is not a "cure" for overcoming anxiety long-term. But it is an effective strategy for now, in the short-term. It's good to use physical activity to control anxiety, and it's healthy for your body, too. This is a tool to help you feel better *now* as you get the "thinking" (cognitive) strategies further and further down into your brain.

This is another paradox: When you feel anxious, panicky, or fearful, don't lay down and give in to anxiety. Instead, get up and get physically active. Do the *opposite* of what you used to do. By getting up and getting active, you are burning off the excessive adrenaline and cortisol, which produced the feelings of anxiety and fear. You will be able to get a handle on your anxiety and calm it down more quickly by using this method.

Anxiety and fear not only stress our bodies out, they make us feel fatigued and tired. As you work against these feelings by exercising away the excessive adrenaline and cortisol, you feel better, and your tiredness and fatigue begin to go away. You weren't fatigued from what you did; the fatigue is a result of your stress level, which is controllable through exercise. It's another paradox. The more active you get, the less tired and fatigued you are. Go ahead and prove this to yourself one day this week.

Getting active isn't the easiest thing in the world to do when you're not in a good mood, and I know that from experience, but it is the only solution for social anxiety at that moment. Don't mope around and throw a pity party for yourself. Instead do the opposite: get up, get active, and exercise the adrenaline and cortisol away. Sometimes this feels hard to do, because anxiety makes you feel immobile, inactive, and exhausted, but think about it for a moment.

We know that anxiety is fueled by the rush of adrenaline, a hormone in our bodies.

The best way to physically get rid of excessive adrenaline is to become physically active and burn it off. If you can get up, move around, and do anything physical (keep the focus on external things, not on yourself), this helps BURN the adrenaline off.

The fear feelings are usually caused by another hormone called cortisol.

The mixture of adrenaline and cortisol is deadly to your mental health.

Cortisol, the stress hormone, is especially controllable by physical activity. Cortisol burns off easier as you get active and exercise – in any way you like.

Any physical activity works: Jumping jacks, running in place, exercising to a DVD, running up and down the stairs, dancing around to music, or lifting weights (they don't have to be heavy – it's the activity that counts).

RATIONAL STATEMENTS:

- *"I'm not going to just sit here and let my anxiety build. I'm going to get up, move around, and get rid of this excessive adrenaline."*

- *"I don't have to live with this stuff right now. I'm going to actively burn it off instead."*

- *"I'm determined to keep moving forward and shrinking the power of this anxiety for good!"*

When in doubt, get active. Move around and exercise. This is not a long-term solution to the problem, but it is a step you can take every day to put you in a better mood and to keep you physically healthy.

Exercise stops excessive worrying and anticipatory anxiety. And anything we can use even temporarily, to banish our anxiety, is good. It is moving us in the right direction.

So, remember: Don't sit still, dwell, or dread. Don't give in to defeat and depression. Instead, get up, get out, and start moving. You can control your anticipatory anxiety by becoming more active.

ACCEPTING MYSELF AS I AM RIGHT NOW

Progress begins when I accept myself.
I accept myself for who I am and what I am.
I accept myself for who I am because acceptance is the pathway to getting better.

I accept myself just the way I am today.
I am a human being and there are parts of my life I want to change.
Just like everyone else, there are parts of my life that cause me trouble and difficulty.

Nevertheless, this does not change the "inner" me.

I accept myself just the way I am today. By accepting myself I am opening the door to healing.

Therefore, I relax. I take a deep breath and peacefully relax.

I am a person with good intentions. There is nothing wrong with the "me" inside – the "intrinsic" me.

I accept myself, problems and all, because the more I accept, the stronger I become.

Acceptance is a powerful process. When I accept myself, I have opened the door for change.

When I let go and accept myself, there is a metamorphosis, a healing power that begins to flow in my life.

As I accept myself for who I am, everything else that is good, healthy, and positive fits naturally and completely into place.

So, I accept myself the way I am today.
As I accept myself, I will begin to change and grow.
Acceptance opens the floodgates of healing and power.
Without acceptance, there is only the struggling and the fighting of the past.

I accept myself for who I am, because as I accept myself, I become a new person.

There is healing in my acceptance. There is power in my acceptance.

Accepting myself means I will not beat myself up anymore.

Others accept me for who I am.

Why shouldn't I accept myself?

I accept myself because I deserve it. I accept myself just as I am so that I can move forward in peace, calmness, strength, and confidence.

Acceptance is the key and the core of my progress. I accept myself and allow this natural pathway to emerge. I accept myself so that I can move forward.

Acceptance is my strength and power.
Acceptance keeps me away from beating myself up and comparing myself to others.
Accepting myself helps me overcome social anxiety.
I accept myself, problems and all, and allow myself to change.

Choose the Easiest Way to Begin Behavioral Therapy

The way we start doing the behavioral therapy, and putting it into place in our life, is by using the step-by-step incremental approach we've been using with the cognitive therapy. We have talked about the importance of repetition, reinforcement and overlearning the cognitive strategies.

We'll do the same thing with the behavioral therapy. Putting the therapy into place and doing it – must be done in the right manner for it to work.

Let me give you some examples of how we want to put the cognitive strategies into place, and why this is the easiest and most effective way to do it:

Let's say you understand why we respond to anxiety by being as calm as possible and not freaking out. Let's also say you realize that your life has been ruled by ANTs for too many years and you are tired of believing ANTs lies that aren't true.

So you begin using slow talk with other people, to cut down your anxiety and increase your calmness in these situations. As you practice this over time, you can eventually use slow talk around people that currently intimidate you, such as bosses and other authority figures.

You are putting slow talk to use in your daily life. You are using it to reduce your anxiety, speak calmly and clearly, and to get your point across intelligibly.

In starting this all out, you need to use slow talk with an easy person, a person that doesn't cause you much anxiety. In any situation, you deliberately choose the *easiest* person to start your behavioral strategy.

The question becomes: **Who is the easiest person to start slow talk with?** You want to start at square one with someone who doesn't cause you much anxiety at all.

You can also choose the easiest situation to start with. If formal meetings seem too difficult to start slow talk in, then start using it at home with your family members or with your friends.

You can use slow talk with anybody at any time. What you are doing now is making sure it is usable and practical, that you can see there are situations right now in which you can use slow talk. If you haven't used slow talk enough, this is the week to work on it every day, gently and calmly, to reduce your anxiety and open yourself up to other people.

By choosing the easiest person in your environment to start this out, you won't feel much anxiety doing it. Use slow talk with the easiest person around, repeat it with the same person if there is any anxiety, and when the anxiety is gone, move up to the next step, which is the next easiest person.

Talk to another person slowly and calmly, and keep using it with this person until you no longer feel anxiety, then move on to the next easiest person.

If you do behavioral therapy systematically like this, you will always be able to do it, and you can always find situations to use it in.

None of us can know everything that's going to happen to us in a day, so it's best to meet daily challenges one by one using this approach.

For example, let's say your supervisor calls a meeting at work and you head down the hallway to the conference room. This involves greeting people and making small talk with them. If your anxiety is high concerning these things, then find an "easy person," maybe someone you already know and feel comfortable around, and make small talk with them using slow talk.

In any new situation, wherever you are, make the choice to talk to other people – but do it by choosing the easiest person in your environment.

Don't charge in to a meeting and head to the company president first, if talking to authority figures causes you anxiety.

Instead, pick an easier person in the room, someone you feel relatively comfortable with, and begin using slow talk with this person. When you no longer feel anxiety with this person, focus on someone else who causes you a little anxiety and talk to them, using slow talk.

This way, you meet each challenge in the present moment and you do not need to avoid anything. You meet your challenges in as non-pressuring way as you can. You look around, find the person that seems easiest to talk to, and make small talk with them, remembering to relax, slow down, and use slow talk.

You choose who you're going to talk to in getting any of the strategies started, and you make the decision of who the next easiest person is.

As you systematically move forward in this fashion, one day you will be able to use slow talk with an authority figure without feeling much anxiety.

We need to begin all our anti-anxiety strategies like this. Choose the easiest person and situation first, and then systematically move up from that point forward.

To summarize,

1. Always choose the easiest person.

2. Don't avoid the situation, but meet it with as much calmness as possible, and take one step at a time.

3. After you've taken the step, give yourself some rational credit. Tell your brain the truth. You made small talk with someone and it went OK. Congratulate yourself for taking it easy and doing it. You didn't avoid it. You calmly responded to anxiety and did it.

4. Then, take another step, with the next easiest person, and move forward from that point.

The Phenomenal Power of One Little Drop of Water

Social anxiety is like the wicked witch of the west. Anxiety seems strong, immovable, and unchangeable right now. But all it takes is one cool, calm drop of water to begin to melt the problem away.

Social anxiety does not have a chance of surviving if you *consistently* drop one cool calm drop of water on it every day.

Anxiety does not like calmness. It can't get any energy from peace. For anxiety to continue to rule your world, you must continually fuel and feed it.

That is how the neural pathway systems in your brain are set up. For anxiety to be in control, it needs the constant reinforcement of negative emotions. The more ANTs, the better. The more fear, the better.

Calmness can change your life

Anxiety needs agitation, fearful expectations, angry responses, irritation, worrying, frustration, depression, and aggression. Anxiety loves it when you become frightened and give in to your negative emotions, because then it gets to rule your life a little longer.

But you know the solution to anxiety is paradoxical. If you respond to anxiety by calming down, by slowing down, by loosening your muscles, and by taking it easy – anxiety has no reinforcement, no energy, and no fuel... nothing for it to feed on.

Anxiety cannot live without reinforcement. If you stop responding to it and reinforcing it, it will shrink and shrink and shrink until it is gone forever.

You will have loved anxiety to death; Death by calmness, rationality, and peace.

Each and every day as you consistently allow yourself to feel peaceful, and you slow any racy irrational thinking down, you are learning a new habit that will put anxiety in its grave.

Then it takes one cool calm drop of water every day. Calmness is the opposite of anxiety. As you approach life more calmly, you will be doing things with less anxiety.

The more you reinforce what is true, the more the neurons will form new pathways and you will begin to think, believe, and feel differently.

A change has already started to occur in your brain. Keep reinforcing it. Continue to move gently forward. Keep up your daily rational reading of the therapy during your thirty minute study time.

We are going to believe the truth. We are tired of believing old, irrational, inaccurate ANTs lies. Our brain is ready to accept the truth.

Social anxiety (the wicked witch) has no chance of survival if you continue moving forward. Drop one cool calming drop of water on her ugly head every day. Respond to the wicked witch (anxiety) with calmness, peace, and rationality – she is not prepared for that and she is not expecting that!

Anxiety cannot continue to exist in the face of the daily reinforcement of one cool calm drop of water. Calmness killed the wicked witch of the west, and it can put an end to social anxiety, too. By developing this new habit of calmness, in any situation, you have put an end to the dominance of irrational social anxiety in your life.

Progressive Muscle Relaxation

Let's learn and use progressive muscle relaxation to take the pressure and stress off ourselves during the day. Progressive muscle relaxation will allow you to *feel* more relaxed and comfortable.

Close your eyes and follow along with the instructions.

As we begin, take a nice deep breath from your abdomen, hold it for a few seconds, and exhale slowly. As you breathe in, notice your lungs filling up with air.

As you exhale, imagine the tension in your body being released and flowing out of your body. Again, inhale… hold it for a few seconds… and exhale. Feel your body relaxing and releasing any tension.

Next, raise your eyebrows as high as you can to tense up your forehead.

Hold this for about five seconds and abruptly release the tension and notice the tightness disappearing. You are releasing and letting go of the tension in your body.

Now smile widely, feeling your mouth and face tense up. Hold for about 5 seconds, and then release it, appreciating the softness in your face.

Next, tighten your eye muscles by holding your eyelids tightly shut. Hold for about 5 seconds, and release.

Keep your eyes closed and gently pull your head back as if you are staring at the ceiling. Do this for 5 seconds, and then release. Feel the tension melt away.

Take one deep breath in… and release it. Your stress and tension is leaving your body… you have control over this.

Let go of all the stress in your entire body. Tense your muscles up, hold for 5 seconds, and let go...

Now, tightly, but without straining, clench your fists and hold them tight for about 5 seconds... and then release.

Notice the relaxation in your hands and arms... You are releasing the tension and stress in your hands and arms...

Now, with your eyes closed, flex your biceps.
Feel that buildup of tension. Visualize the muscle tightening.
Hold it for about 5 seconds, and then let go. Enjoy the feeling of relaxation and limpness in your arms.

Breathe in deeply... and exhale. All tension and stress is leaving your body.
Now extend your arms out straight, locking your elbows to tighten your triceps. Hold it for 5 seconds, and then bring your arms back to rest. Feel the tension evaporate.

Notice the relaxation in your arms and in your muscles. You have released the tension and stress in that part of your body.

Now lift your shoulders up as if they could touch your ears. Hold it for 5 seconds, and quickly release, feeling their heaviness disappear.

Relax completely and let the stress go. Your shoulders are loose and relaxed. You can see this in your mind's eye...

Pull your shoulders back, and tense your upper back, as if to make your shoulder blades touch. Hold for about 5 seconds and release.
Notice the feeling of relaxation in your back.
Next, tighten your chest by taking a deep breath in, hold for about 5 seconds, and exhale, releasing all tension into the air.

Now tighten the muscles in your stomach by pulling it in... Hold for 5 seconds, and release.

Gently raise and push your lower back forward. Your stomach is in the air and your lower back muscles are tense. Hold for 5 seconds, and let go.

Feel the limpness in your upper body as you let go of all the tension and stress. Tighten your buttocks. Hold for 5 seconds, and then release. All the tension and stress is gone.

Tighten your thighs by pressing your knees together, as if you were holding a penny between them. Hold it for 5 seconds, and then let go.

Now flex your feet, pulling your toes towards you and feeling the tension in your lower legs. Hold for 5 seconds, and relax. Feel the weight of your legs sinking down.

Imagine a wave of peace and relaxation slowly spreading throughout your body, beginning at your head and moving all the way down to your feet.

Feel the weight of your relaxed body.

Breathe in deeply for 5 seconds, and exhale.

Let all the tension and stress go. See the wave of relaxation and calmness engulfing you and releasing all the stress from your body.

Relax... Take it easy... Let go of all the tension so that you feel very loose and light. Now slowly open your eyes gradually and peacefully, and notice how calm and relaxed you feel.

Progressive muscle relaxation should be started at home, but after doing it several times, you'll remember a few muscle groups that you can relax. You'll be able to use progressive muscle relaxation in everyday life situations, with a little bit of adaptation.

Preparation (Review) for Permanently Changing our Thoughts and Beliefs:
Replacing ANTs Thoughts with Automatic Rational Thinking

We are now ready to replace our irrational thoughts and beliefs with rational thoughts and beliefs, but we can't *replace* irrational beliefs until we have caught and stopped them:

So, here is a very short review of how to catch and label automatic negative thoughts. By now, you should be pretty good at catching automatic negative thoughts and beliefs that run through your head. Remember, catching them is not enough.

The brain, because it is a neutral organ, must be made aware that we do not like, and we do not want, to have these automatic negative thoughts and beliefs. So, we need to tell the brain this by saying something like

- ➢ "STOP! I don't like those automatic negative thoughts. They're not healthy or helpful to me. They're not even true."

- ➢ I will get up, get active, and do something to get my mind away from the vicious cycle of automatic negative thinking."

In addition, we label these thoughts and beliefs as untrue, as inaccurate, and as lies. Lies that try to bully us into staying stuck in our irrational thoughts and beliefs forever.

These irrational beliefs are not going to win. Because of your daily effort in reading over and refreshing yourself with the solutions, you are allowing your brain to change and to become more rational.

It's necessary to catch, stop, and label automatic negative thinking as being irrational and as being wrong. The end result is in no longer having automatic negative thoughts occur.

How can we get to this place? That is the topic of our next handout.

Right now, we can catch, label, and dismiss our automatic negative thoughts, plus we've told our brain that we do not want to think this way any longer. We want the automatic rational thinking to begin.

We will be replacing ANTs thoughts with rational thoughts next

So...

1. Catch the ANTs Thought

2. Tell the brain they are negative thoughts and you don't like them

3. Use distractions or do something constructive to get your mind off ANTs

4. Label the ANTs as liars, untruthful, bullies, and irrational

5. New step: We are now moving to the next step, which is replacing old irrational thinking with automatic rational thinking

We will be changing not only our negative thoughts, but our entire belief system.

We will do it in a step-by-step manner, because that's the way the brain works.

Turning the Tables on the ANTs, Part I:
Establishing New Realistic and Rational Thinking

The brain is not designed like a computer. It is made up of hundreds of billions of nerve cells that conduct electricity and release chemicals.

Every time you replace an ANTs thought with an accurate, rational thought, you are literally, physically, altering the circuitry of your brain.

You are the only one who can change your brain chemistry and your brain's circuitry – by no longer accepting the poisonous ANTS thoughts and beliefs.

You choose the do the opposite instead: to focus, pay attention to, and believe rational, accurate thoughts. You are going to use your positive emotions to become more rational in your thinking.

Most of us have spent years and years being controlled by ANTS – but now it's time to change our brain circuitry for good. There's only one way to stop these automatic negative thoughts – and that is by surrounding ourselves with rational, accurate, realistic thinking.

Step #1: I Can Change Because the Brain is Wired to Change

If I learned to have worrying and anxiety-ridden thoughts, then I can learn to have rational and calming thoughts.

None of us was born with social anxiety. Since we weren't born with social anxiety and the automatic negative thoughts that accompany it, our thoughts are not permanently set in stone.

You can learn to think and feel differently because the brain is malleable and changeable.

Step #2: Let's Turn that ANTS Thought Around

How do we actually change our beliefs so that the rational beliefs begin to occur automatically, without us having to think about it?

The answer is gradually, and by being precise; we are going to turn the tables on the ANTs slowly. This is another process – it is something we do deliberately, over a period of time.

Let me explain this to you in detail…

If you have anticipatory anxiety about an upcoming situation, you turn the tables on the ANTs by thinking about what the rational response would be.

Here's how to do it: If you're anxious and worried about an upcoming event that has caused you anxiety in the past, you take the worry and fear, and turn it upside down by responding differently than you have in the past. You calm yourself down instead of worrying, doubting, and fearing. You relax your muscles, loosen up, and take a deep breath. You accept yourself and the calmness within you.

Then, you say to yourself:

> ➢ "You know, being the center of attention is not something I like and it is not fun. It has caused me a lot of anxiety in the past… BUT maybe it's not as bad as I made it out to be. Maybe I exaggerate it in my mind and blow it way out of proportion."

Instead of worrying, we begin changing our beliefs by saying rational things to ourselves, and by refusing to go negative anymore.

You just made a rational statement about being the center of attention, and then said, "But maybe it's not as bad as I made it out to be…" and then made another rational statement: "Maybe I exaggerate it in my mind and blow it way out of proportion."

The brain will always accept rational statements. It will not accept highly positive statements like: "I love being the center of attention and I'm going to be the center of attention everywhere I go today! Woohoo!" Hence, we will never psych ourselves up or reinforce highly positive statements that are pretty irrational in themselves.

Your brain cannot be psyched up into believing a statement like that.

Instead, we will keep our replacement thoughts rational, and, by being rational, our brain will believe what we say.

We need to be careful about strong negative, absolute words, such as hate, can't, or never. Your brain latches on to these strong, absolute words, and remembers and believes them more easily. So let's begin eliminating them from what we say to ourselves.

For example, saying "I can't be the center of attention" only reinforces your fear and makes it come true.

It's better to say, "Right now, I don't think I can handle being the center of attention. But maybe, as I continue to work on my therapy, I'll be better able to handle it."

By saying that to yourself, you have interrupted the old fire-and wire connections in the brain, and your brain is able to accept what you said because what you said is rational.

Take away the big, bold negative statements, and *replace* them with conditional or neutral language. Catch and stop yourself from saying big absolute words like this:

"I **can't** do that. It causes too much anxiety..."
"I'll **never** be able to give a presentation..."
"**No** way!"
"I **hate** being the center of attention"
"Talking in public **always** makes me anxious."

You need to catch and stop all the big negative absolute words like these, and make a rational statement to yourself, out loud, instead.

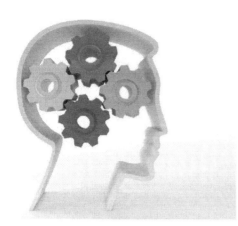

Instead of "I can't go to the party because of my anxiety," say instead, "I feel that the party will cause me anxiety right now, but maybe I'm over-exaggerating and worrying about it too much. Maybe I make the situation scarier because I keep saying "I can't do it." Maybe I can't do it today, but maybe I will be ready to go to a party in a month or two."

The brain believes what you repeatedly tell it, so let's get into the habit of minimizing our automatic negative thoughts instead of magnifying them even further.

The first part of turning the tables on the ANTs is to stop, catch, and turn those big, bold absolute negative words around. We are replacing those negative beliefs with neutral, rational beliefs instead.

There is great power in the words we use. We want to stay away from negative, defeatist words because if we keep using them, they become self-fulfilling prophecies and our life never changes.

Maybe you've set your brain up for anxiety by constantly reminding yourself that you hate this upcoming event, and you "know" it is going to cause you lots of fear and anxiety ahead of time.

So, maybe there's some wiggle room here to stay rational with your thinking and move a little bit forward, too. You want to go rational with your words, and stay away from big, bold, absolute negative words.

You need to stop saying "I hate this," or "I can't do" something because of my anxiety.

Instead, by staying rational, you can say that "in the past, I haven't liked it, but maybe now, because I know some anti-anxiety strategies, it might not be as bad as it once was."

Think about this: It may not be accurate for you to keep saying that being the center attention or making a presentation will kill you anymore. Maybe you have blown the situation out of proportion. You still don't like being the center of attention, but maybe you've made it out to be worse than it really is. Maybe... Perhaps... or it could be that you've blown your fears up, out of proportion to reality.

Absolute words and phrases to eliminate from our speech:

"I HATE doing answering the phone..."

"I CAN'T run the group meeting..."

"It's IMPOSSIBLE for me to talk to my supervisor..."

"My anxiety's TOO HIGH for me to talk to strangers..."

"I'll NEVER be able to give a presentation..."

"Other people ALWAYS stress me out and cause me anxiety..."

"I can NEVER do that because of my anxiety"

"I've tried everything. I'll NEVER get over social anxiety."

"Giving a presentation is IMPOSSIBLE. It causes me too much stress and grief."

"I WON'T ever be able to do that."

"That ALWAYS scares me."

"I hate making introductions. They always cause me terrible amounts of anxiety." Keep in mind that your brain believes everything it hears repeatedly, especially if you are saying it.

If you say, "I can't do that," your brain believes you, and makes it come true. You can't do it because you've told yourself repeatedly you can't do it. Your brain *believes* you because it has caused so much anxiety in the past. When you say you can't do it enough, you brainwash yourself into believing that you can't do it.

That's why it's important to eliminate the big, bold, absolute negative words from your self-talk. What you say to yourself repeatedly is believed by the brain. If the brain believes it, it will be true for you.

Whatever you strongly believe about yourself comes true.

De-Stressing Strategies

Don't take life so seriously.

Lighten up and take it easy.

This is NOT a life and death experience.

This is NOT an either/or, black or white situation.

Take a deep breath – inhale deeply – and then exhale.

The world is not going to end over this... guaranteed!

There is humor in almost everything.

Paradoxical Strategy: Carry your worries out to illogical, ridiculous lengths and then laugh about them.

Don't listen to anxiety feelings – they are ANTs lies. Listen and tell yourself the rational truth.

All you can do is your best – and then forget about it.

The way I feel today is not going to influence the fate of the world today, tomorrow, or next week, let alone in the millennia to come.

It's no big deal!

My worry is not going to make the situation better... it will only make me feel worse...

I am who I am and I'm human. So is everyone else. We all make mistakes.

Making mistakes is the only way we learn to do things in a better way. We make a lot of progress when we're making mistakes.

My own worst enemy is avoidance.

Rest, relax, accept, fall back into the flow of the moment. Let calmness and peace do the "work" for you. Don't pile pressure on yourself.

When you feel anxious and stressed, stop what you're doing momentarily, slow your thinking down, loosen your muscles, and deliberately take your time.

Remember the story of the tortoise and the hare? The rabbit rushes faster and hops around in circles, but the slow and steady turtle stays on course and wins the race.

I choose to be consistent, stay on course, and overcome social anxiety.

Quick PMR:
Using Progressive Muscle Relaxation in Public

In public, social situations when other people are around, you can use a modified form of progressive muscle relaxation to feel calmer and more comfortable. Here are some things you can do:

Take a deep breath through your abdomen, and exhale slowly. Notice your abdominal muscles loosening up and relaxing.

As you exhale, imagine the tension in your body being released and flowing out. Now inhale again... hold this for a few seconds... and exhale...

Feel your body relaxing and releasing any tenseness.

Change your facial expression naturally so that you can let go of any tenseness in your face or forehead... Notice how it feels different – you are releasing and letting go of all the tension in your face.

When you can, close your eyes briefly... As you open them, notice the stress and tension leaving your eyes and face and allow yourself to feel the calmness wash over you.

When it seems natural, look up at something high for a second or two, and then bring your head back down to normal.

Notice you were using your shoulder and neck muscles, and now you are releasing any tightness or stress you were holding there. You can feel a sense of **relaxation** as the muscles in your neck and shoulders loosen up.

Take one deep breath in... and release it. Any stress and tension in your body is leaving right now... you have control over allowing this to happen.

Let go of all the stress, anywhere in your body. Now, without straining or being seen, gently clench one or both of your fists, and release it...

Notice the relaxation in your hands and arms... you are gently releasing the tension and stress all the way through your arms to your hands.

Now, gently flex your biceps so that it's not noticed. Let go, and enjoy the feeling of relaxation and the limpness in your arm.

Breathe in deeply... and exhale. The tension and stress is leaving your body.

If you're standing, keep your posture straight, but loosen up your muscles so that you can feel a little bit of relaxation. Feel all tension and stress leaving your body...

If you're sitting, lean back completely into the chair, and let go of any tightness or tension you may feel...

Let go of any stress around your stomach area... relax your stomach muscles and let all the tension go.

Now flex your feet, pulling your toes towards you and feeling the tension in your lower legs. Hold it for about 5 seconds, and then relax.

Now imagine a wave of relaxation slowly spreading through your body, beginning at your head and moving all the way down to your feet.

Breathe this relaxation in deeply, and exhale. See the wave of relaxation and calmness engulfing you, and releasing all the stress.

These are **adaptations of the formal progressive muscle relaxation** you do when you're alone.

There are other ways of loosening up your muscles and releasing muscle tension, so keep your mind open to other ways of relaxing and feeling comfortable, regardless of how many people are in the situation with you. You can adapt most progressive muscle relaxation techniques and use them in your daily life.

Turning the Tables on ANTS, Part II:
Keep Turning Those Irrational Thoughts Around

We don't have to live through every single situation we fear, and gently calm ourselves down to get better.

Learning to calm down and relax in one anxiety situation *bleeds over* or spreads into other situations where we experience anxiety, making this turning-the-tables approach the most effective and quickest way to get better. Plus, it's the only strategy that works to make permanent changes in the brain.

The solution to changing our old thinking patterns and beliefs is to...

1. Slow yourself down; take your time and don't rush yourself.

2. Relax, and realize the situation you're in is not the end of the world.

3. Think clearly and rationally to yourself; use "slow thinking."

4. Face situations as they occur, calmly, one situation at a time. You will not be overwhelmed with anxiety when you deal with life in this way.

Facing your fears in the wrong manner is like slamming into a brick wall

5. Notice the bleed-over effect. If you feel less anxious making introductions than you used to, you will also feel less anxious in other situations, too, without needing to work on each and every anxiety-provoking situation.

The brain will believe how you interpret an event because of what you *say* about it, whether you're being rational or not. If you keep saying you *hate* something, the brain accepts what you say, and causes you to be fearful of the event you hate. Because of your belief system, you feel anxious every time you do the "hated" event.

Every time you're asked to introduce yourself, you experience fear and anxiety because you keep saying you "hate" it, even though you are doing a calm, professional job at making introductions.

This is a big problem, because at this rate, even if you become the best introduction-giver in the world, you are still going to be fearful when you do it, and you're still going to hate making introductions.

Why? Because you are not turning the tables on the ANTs and replacing those bold absolute negative words with neutral, rational words.

We need to be rational with ourselves and remember the brain bases its beliefs on what we repeatedly say.

We should say to ourselves, "Introductions used to cause me anxiety. But, I think I did an OK job at it the last time. I relaxed as much as I could and I used slow talk. Maybe if I keep doing introductions like this, using these cognitive strategies, introductions will feel easier. I'm not positive of that yet, but it could happen that way. Maybe someday I'll even feel comfortable doing them."

Notice, you are being rational without being ridiculously positive.

You are breaking up the old wire-and-fire connections in the brain that lead to fear. As you interrupt these old associations, you are allowing your brain's neurons to associate with other neurons that carry rational thoughts and beliefs.

If we continue to tell our brains that we hate to make introductions or we can't give a presentation – then our performance may get better, but we will still feel fearful and anxious about it.

It's time to turn the tables on the ANTs. Your brain will believe a lie if you tell it a lie, such as "I am horrible at making introductions." That's not really true, but you have made it come true because you've said it so very often.

Tell your brain the truth instead – Say to yourself, "I did OK at making introductions today" – and gradually, as you tell your brain the truth, your beliefs and emotions will follow along.

The brain is a fascinating organ. It is neutral in the sense that it doesn't know what's healthy or not for you in different situations in life. It doesn't necessarily help you get better like we all wish it did. For example, the brain does not automatically help us figure out how to overcome social anxiety. It was as uneducated as we are.

The brain only knows something because you tell it something. The brain knows things because you open yourself up to new ideas, concepts, and values. You are the one in control of how the brain treats you.

As we tell the brain to focus on strategies that help us get better, then the brain will do what you ask of it. It's only when you tell the brain what you want, relative to social anxiety, that the brain begins to seek out answers for you, and moves your life in the direction you suggest.

The brain, by itself, is a neutral object. You tell it what's good for you and what isn't. The brain believes everything you say to it repeatedly.

Since the brain is this powerful, let's make sure our self-talk is accurate and rational.

You are in total control of your own self-talk, and thus, you are in control of what your brain believes and what your future will be like.

You need to tell the brain what's rational and what isn't, and you need to reinforce whatever is the rational truth. Throughout history, people have believed things that weren't true, yet they were willing to die for their beliefs because they believed them so strongly.

They thought and said something over and over again, and made this belief true for them. They repeated and reinforced something irrational and untrue, yet they continued to strongly believe it. Therefore, it was true for them.

This is a trap all of us fell into in the past. We have unwanted negative thoughts and beliefs – and we think they are true. So we act in accordance with our beliefs, even though they are irrational. When we have social anxiety we believe that we're being judged and evaluated by others, but this belief may not be true. We do not want to believe things that may be inaccurate and irrational.

Now that we know better, we worked on catching and stopping our irrational negative thoughts, and replacing them with new rational beliefs. We also need to keep our mind open to new interpretations and viewpoints, instead of keeping it closed due to fear and anxiety.

Now, when we do something that was difficult for us to do in the past, it is important that we notice it, give ourselves credit for doing it, and then turn the tables on the ANTs.

For example, you can say, "Yes, that was anxiety-causing for me, but I did it by slowing down and remaining calm as possible and I'm glad I did it. It wasn't as bad as I thought it would be. In fact, I might feel less and less anxiety every time I do it."

If you keep your brain open and use neutral self-talk, the brain will gradually change your thoughts about yourself, and the situation at hand. You are replacing old irrational beliefs with new rational beliefs.

You will be turning the tables on the ANTs by breaking up your rigid ANTs thinking patterns. Your thoughts and emotions will begin to change as a result – and the situation will no longer be as anxiety causing as it once was.

Here's another example:

When you catch yourself saying,
"Oh, no! I hate to do this!", see if you can turn that ANT around. Say to yourself, "I used to hate doing this, but it's a little easier for me now. It's not as monstrous and anxiety-provoking as I thought it was."

That is a very mild, beginning neutral statement, but it moves us forward – away from using absolute words like "hate" and "can't" and statements like "I'll never be able to do that!" The more you say you hate to do something, the more you will hate to do it.

The brain hears, understands, and believes anything that you say repeatedly, so let's not sabotage our lives by telling ourselves we can't do things, or that we hate to do them.

➢ I'll turn the tables on the ANTs instead by saying: "Maybe I can do more things than I give myself credit for, and maybe I don't hate them as much as I once did. In fact, now it's not that big a deal at all. I guess I've been blowing things out of proportion."

Stop yourself from making rigid absolute negative statements, and then make a more realistic, neutral statement instead.

To change our irrational thoughts and beliefs (ANTs):
Go Conditional With Your Thoughts and Beliefs

You need to tell your brain the rational truth. For example:

"I don't like making presentations. It's caused me great anxiety in the past."

That is a rational statement, so it's fine to say it.

But, do not turn it in a negative direction. Stay away from words like horrible ("Giving presentations is just horrible!"), hate ("I hate making a presentation"), can't ("I just can't make a presentation"), always ("Presentations always cause me anxiety"), and never ("I'll never be able to do that!")

It makes a big difference what you say repeatedly to yourself. The brain will notice what you say and will believe you. Stay rational so that your thoughts and beliefs can gradually change.

Keep in mind that your brain does change with time. The understanding of "brain plasticity" allows us to discard old, irrational thoughts, and start believing new, rational thoughts, one step at a time. So, be honest in your statement, like above, but do not go negative with it.

A better – more rational – way of framing the statement would be:

"I don't like making presentations. It's caused me high amounts of anxiety in the past. But maybe I learned a few strategies that will calm me down now. Maybe it will be easier this time because I can slow myself down. Perhaps I've been blowing my fears out of proportion to the actual danger involved. I don't think this is a life-or-death experience."

Use conditional or neutral words instead of going negative – like you did in the past. Use conditional words instead of going silly-positive, because that's a leap that's too far, too fast for your brain to believe.

Your brain won't accept the 100% positive statement ("I love public speaking!") because it isn't rational… it's outlandishly positive, and the brain won't believe it. That statement is a joke.

So, if we really want to change our negative thoughts and beliefs, we need to make **neutral or conditional statements** about situations that cause us anxiety. "Maybe I'll have less anxiety about public speaking…" "Perhaps it will be easier for me because I've learned to slow down."

Stay rational with what you say. Don't reinforce your current irrational beliefs, and don't go ridiculously positive. Use neutral or conditional words to keep it sounding realistic to you.

**Examples of conditional words to use to
break up our old negative fire-wire connections:**

maybe
could
possibly
perhaps
might
sometimes

Neutral Word	Example
Maybe	Maybe it won't be as bad as it was before.
Could	It could be that I am handling anxiety better now. I can slow myself down and get rational faster.
Just possibly	Just possibly, I have made some progress. Maybe this isn't the end of the world. Just possibly I will feel less anxious by using slow talk.

Perhaps	Perhaps I am getting better, so that I'll have less anxiety. I'm not sure yet, but perhaps I can remember to slow down and loosen my muscles first.
Who knows?	I am keeping my brain OPEN to new thoughts and beliefs. I will not close it off in negative all-or-nothing thinking. Absolute thinking never helps. If I allow my brain to discover what is rational, it will do that – provided that I tell it to do it.

Changing our belief system is a process: it takes time and patience, but it happens.

- Your brain will accept what's rational if you keep an open mind.

- You can change your thoughts and beliefs by staying rational and using conditional words to keep you rational.

- Stay away from automatic negative thinking, but don't go ridiculously positive. This is not genuine "positivity," and the brain will not accept this statement.

- Use neutral statements and keep your mind open. Your brain will figure out what's rational over time.

Are You on the Right Track With Your Comprehensive CBT?
Two Major Symptoms of Social Anxiety Give Us the Answer

If an activity causes us self-consciousness, or causes us to be afraid of becoming the center of attention, then the activity is something we need to work on in our gentle, step-by-step approach.

Any behavioral experiment we do that has the potential to decrease either variable, decreases the other variable, too.

Researchers say that reducing your feelings of anxiety in one situation of your life, "bleeds over" into other situations in your life. If you feel less anxious about introducing yourself to other people, you will also feel a reduction in anxiety when mingling with people, standing up for yourself, or giving a presentation.

Cognitive-behavioral therapy works because we overlearn it. We deliberately go past – or "overdo" – the strategy that helps reduce anxiety. In research on learning, this process is called "overlearning." If you overlearn the cognitive strategies and apply them, the brain's neural circuitry is tighter and stronger.

To overlearn, we deliberately go farther with our strategies, at home or in a social anxiety therapy group, than we do in regular life. We repeat the activity, reinforce it, and do it again and again, until it no longer causes us anxiety.

"Overlearning" means we run the activity into the ground, so that it is learned, relearned, and overlearned. This is how new habits are generated.

Overlearning is the most effective, and only way, to make sure we are permanently "getting" the cognitive and the behavioral therapy into our brains so that change can occur.

In the series, everything we do, week in and week out, is gently working on these two major symptoms of social anxiety: **(a) self-consciousness, and (b) fear of being the center of attention.**

Most of the strategies we employ are interrelated, and one strategy makes another strategy stronger and easier to do. It is overlearning and overdoing the cognitive and behavioral strategies that are the keys to solving these two primary symptoms of social anxiety.

So, in context of what you're working on, it doesn't really make much difference which anxiety trigger seems strongest or most relevant to you right now. As long as you are working on becoming less self-conscious or you are working on reducing your fear of being the center of attention, you are on the right track.

We wouldn't have time to address all our anxiety triggers anyway. If we addressed every last symptom of social anxiety specifically, we could find additional fears to put on our list for the next fifty years. What makes behavioral therapy work is that when you feel less anxious in one area, it spreads over into other areas.

So, if you are working on an activity that

(a) reduces your self-consciousness, or
(b) reduces your fear of being the center of attention,

then you are directly and specifically working against all symptoms of social anxiety. You are on the right track in the process of overcoming social anxiety.

Cognitive Distortions

Here's the type of thinking to catch and stop:

1. Should/Must Thinking: Using words like "should," "must," "can't," and "have to" implies that we live by rigid, pressuring rules in our lives. Pressuring ourselves like this only increases our anxiety.

Because of the pressure involved, holding yourself accountable to these "should's," "musts," and "have to's" will backfire on you and cause you additional anxiety. Dr. Albert Ellis taught his clients that they shouldn't "should" on themselves, and he was right.

Examples of should/must thinking:

- "I *should* finish that work project today. I'm not going home until it's done, even if I'm here until midnight."
- "I *must* do a perfect job or I'll just give up."
- "It *must* be done this way. There's no other way to get it done."
- "I *can't* talk to the boss. I might as well not even try."
- "I *can't* be in charge of that meeting. They'll notice my nervousness and anxiety, and my hands and arms will start shaking."
- "I *have to* overcome social anxiety right away. I have to do it this month so I can start out my new job without any anxiety."

2. Overgeneralizing: Words like "always," "never," "everyone," and "no one" are inaccurate, and much of the time we use these words to beat ourselves up.

Examples of overgeneralizing:

- "Everyone is staring at me, and I know they don't like me."

- "I feel like I'm being inspected. *Everyone* is looking at me and expecting me to make a fool of myself."
- "*No one* likes me. I don't have a friend in the world. I've *never* known how to make friends."

3. Magnification: We have the capability of turning everything into a catastrophe, or emergency. We blow things out of proportion. A small, innocent remark is taken the wrong way and we let it explode on us, and dwell on it for days, weeks, and months.

Example of Magnification:

"My supervisor said he wasn't sure if my approach was the right one. OMG! He doesn't appreciate all the time I've spent getting this company back on track. He's putting me down in public, in front of everyone else! If he doesn't appreciate everything I've done for him, then I'm going to quit!"

Your friend made an off-the-cuff comment that everyone thought was funny. For some reason, you thought the comment was directed at you and that everyone was laughing at you.

"How could she have said something so horrible?" you cry. "I am always nice to her." Meanwhile, your friend has no idea that you misinterpreted her comment, and you are too afraid to directly address the problem with her.

4. Minimization: We minimize the good feedback that we receive. If we are complimented, we tend to dismiss or discount the positive comment. It's like we're saying the other person is a liar. The real reason we do this is that we can't believe that we've done something well. It's a new belief that doesn't correspond to our old beliefs about ourselves. In the past, we have minimized heartfelt genuine comments from other people.

Example of minimization:

Jacob: "I enjoyed your talk."

Your response: "Thank you." (You are thinking this couldn't be true, that Jacob is trying to be nice, or trying to gain your favor, or maybe he feels sorry for you. It's not possible he is being sincere.)

Jacob: "That was an interesting experience you told us about."

Is this hard to accept? The person was sincere and meant it. Is it still hard to accept? Is Jacob a liar?

5. Mind Reading: We make assumptions about what other people are thinking based on little or no evidence. Sometimes, it's the expression on their face, or their general demeanor, or how quiet they are. We don't have enough evidence to make accurate judgments about what other people are thinking inside.

Examples of Mind Reading:

"I know Jennifer doesn't like me because she never smiles at me."
(How do you know what's going on inside Jennifer's head?)

"Josh dislikes me because I did better on that project than he did. He's just a jealous guy."
In reality, Josh may not know how he did on the project, and making judgments based on one experience is not rational.

6. Personalization: We internalize or personalize things that happen around us. If someone is silent, we assume they're mad at us, when they may be thinking about a problem at home, a party that's coming up, or their grandmother who is in the hospital.

We sometimes personalize, magnify, and overgeneralize all at once, to our own detriment. A neutral comment that was not supposed to mean anything at all is something we can misinterpret, get offended by, and take personally, like it was said directly to hurt us.

7. Emotional Reasoning: Watch out for reasoning based on emotion. Take the emotion out of the way you interpret life. Then, see what's left. Stay as emotionally rational with yourself as you can. We can't make decisions based

on how we feel at a given moment and expect to overcome social anxiety. Our decisions about what to do must come from rational thinking.

The use of emotions to evaluate and judge a situation, belief, or event skews the intention. We should quiet ourselves down, move into the "peace" zone, and then reassess the situation. It is likely our emotions were not telling us the truth.

When we calm down and look at the situation calmly and rationally, using common sense, our brain quiets down, and we won't judge things according to the way we feel at the time.

Take the emotion out of the situation. Then, calmly see if this changes your perspective.

8. All or Nothing Thinking: The tendency to make judgments in stark black and white, either/or, "one or the other" terms. Something is either all good or all bad. In life, almost everything has shades of gray, due to the context of the situation and the intent of the person. All this needs to be understood, to come up with a rational conclusion.

Explanation of all-or-nothing thinking:

All or nothing thinking is not good for us, especially when it comes to turning the tables on the ANTs and seeing things from different points of view. We learned to use neutral words like "maybe," "somewhat," "could be," and "possibly," to break up, or interrupt, our habits of automatic negative thinking.

We want to notice the pattern of cognitive distortions we have left, stop them, calm ourselves down, and become rational with ourselves. This is done by eliminating emotional reasoning, and considering different perspectives on the situation.

Acting on cognitive distortions leads to pain and misery. Distorted thinking is an old brain habit that we interrupt and break up so that we can see what is rational and true. Emotional reasoning keeps us away from our goal.

➢ The first thing I'll do when making an assessment or judgment is to slow down and not react. I need to look at the issue from every different perspective, and make sure my emotions are not driving my interpretations. My rational assessment is accurate and by using it I am breaking the habit of irrational thinking and cognitive distortions.

Small Talk is "Small Talk" Because it's Small

It is ordinary, common, mundane, not-that-important talk... it's "no big deal" talk...

You may run in to your neighbor on the street and exchange one or two sentences. You may be in a room with co-workers getting ready for a meeting to start, you may be sitting in a classroom and exchanging greetings and making small talk with other students.

Small talk is not something "important" or "earth shattering." In fact, people engage in small talk to be friendly, not because the conversation has any depth or meaning.

We'll look at small talk as a way of being friendly. Friendliness is a cognitive strategy we can use to reduce and eliminate anxiety. The strategy of being friendly produces a paradoxical outcome. You think that being friendly is difficult, requires work, and is stressful, when actually the opposite is true. If you take the initiative, are friendly, and talk to another person first, you will feel anxiety go down almost immediately.

When you act, your feelings follow.

Act by being friendly. Say something. If you say something, your anxiety will go down, but if you remain silent, you give anxiety a chance to rise.

Making small talk is a human custom that shows others that you're "there" in the present moment, and you're a friendly person. What you actually say is not that important. Your willingness to be open and make small talk with others is what's important.

You do not need to be entertaining or humorous, or witty and charming, so take the pressure off yourself.

If you think you have nothing to say, that's because you have been telling this to yourself for years and years. Actually, you can talk, and you have plenty of things you can talk about.

Looking at this rationally, all of us have plenty to say. In fact, the quieter you've been in your life, the more likely it is you have a LOT to say ☺

If you haven't made small talk much, you'll find that getting into the habit is relatively easy, takes the pressure off yourself, and doesn't allow feelings of self-consciousness to intrude. It will put you in a better mood and make your day better.

Small talk is a form of greeting in most cultures. You simply say, "How are you?" and then talk about the weather, an upcoming event, or an activity like entertainment or sports. It's an acknowledgement of the other person's presence.

For example:

What kind of a dog is that?

I thought the sun would never come out.

Does the bus run by your house?

I work three miles from here.

It's been hot lately, hasn't it?

Any little thing you say is "small talk."

Small talk is small talk because it's small. No one will remember what you said when you made small talk yesterday. What you said is not earth-shattering. It's just a friendly, pleasant way to live in the present moment. Open yourself up to the idea of making a little small talk with others.

Taking the initiative, saying hello to people first, and making comments to them puts you in charge and cuts down your anxiety immediately.

So, when you see a neighbor outside you can say, "Hello! It sure has been hot, hasn't it?" As your neighbor responds, you do what you came out to do, and the small talk is over before you realize it.

At work or in school, people make comments about what's going to be on the next test, how you studied for it, what the boss expects from the team today, or what one of your co-workers did last night.

The secret to small talk is to simply open your mouth and say something. Talk about the weather, or sports, or something else that people generally share. Small talk is never lengthy, and you can say the same thing all day, since each time you make small talk you're talking to a different person.

There are additional reasons to feel good about small talk.

Dr. Viveka Adelswärd, linguist and Professor Emeritus in Communication at Linköping University, studies ways people understand and misunderstand each other in every day conversation.

"Small talk provides us with lots of information and confirms our social group affiliation," notes the professor.

She explains that conversational patterns can't be learned theoretically by taking a class or by formal instruction. People have to *participate* in conversations to be able to understand how taking turns during a conversation operates, how to keep the conversation going, noticing transitions from subject to subject, or when someone wants to end the conversation.

"On an individual level, small talk also fulfills another function," she says. "We formulate our thoughts and ideas while we are talking."

This basic research reinforces that while we are making small talk, the brain generates more thoughts and help us with our conversation. But it's only after we start talking that this happens.

Making small talk encourages the understanding of why we say what we say when we say it.

Until we actually make small talk with others, we don't feel the naturalness of doing it. Adults pick up conversational cues very quickly, even if they haven't had much experience in making small talk.

Children rely on verbal communication almost entirely, report researchers at the University of Washington. For young children, all talk is inherently "small."

An intensive study reveals children require live, back-and-forth interaction with adults in order to effectively learn communication. The conversation need not be meaningful, but it does need to be reciprocal.

This just means that when you engage in small talk with other people, and they respond to you, you are learning something from the situation that will help you for the rest of your life.

Dr. Adelswärd wrote that people thrive when they make small talk, because of the imperceptible things they learn, the continuing communication it allows, and the feelings of happiness and joy that go along with it.

We don't actually know what we're going to say until we say something in these situations. The fear of saying something small can be a major block to our progress, but you can gently overcome it by greeting someone, keeping yourself calm, and using slow talk.

Even though it's not readily apparent, small talk has great additional benefits in helping us communicate better with people and feel better about ourselves because of it.

Turning the Tables on ANTS, Part III:
Or Your Brain Hears and Believes Everything You (Repeatedly) Say

Everything you say is "interpreted" literally by the brain.

That is, if we tell ourselves that a particular situation makes us fearful, then we are reinforcing the idea that when we are in that situation, we will be afraid. If we continue to reinforce our anxieties, the real life fears that we face will grow stronger.

That's why, in the past, we may have been exposed to many highly-anxiety arousing situations – and even though we've gone through them hundreds of times before, this "exposure" to feared situations did not make us feel less anxious. We were still just as afraid of the situation after we did it the 100th time as we were when we did it the first.

In order to get over these big fears, we need to begin to change our thoughts and our language about what we're doing behaviorally (or how we are acting).

For example, speaking in public is something most people with social anxiety find very difficult to do. But, if we constantly remind ourselves (and our brain) that we think it is horrible, scary, and anxiety-provoking, then it will always be horrible, scary, and anxiety-provoking.

We are reinforcing our own fears and making them stronger every time we repeat this statement to ourselves.

We are sabotaging ourselves and our own best interests. Why should we do that?

It's because we've never been told this before, and we've never fully realized what we were doing to ourselves.

Most situations in life are not really that scary: we have just interpreted them that way for a long period of time and they have settled deeply in our brains; it *seems* like they are scary. So now, as we continue to get better, we are learning to interpret these situations more rationally and realistically.

A rational statement and viewpoint about a situation eventually changes the old ANTS feelings – and then anxiety can no longer get in the way to disrupt our lives.

- Turn the tables on those ANTs
- Your brain hears everything you say
- Make sure you are telling it the truth
- Make sure you are being realistic and accurate
- Don't say you "can't" do something, because maybe in the future you can

Tell your brain the truth. Turn the tables on the ANTs. Stop sabotaging your life. Whatever you say, your brain will hear. Whatever your brain hears, it will believe. Your brain interprets things quite literally, even when you're being irrational.

If you say and repeat for years that you hate something, your brain believes that you hate it. You reinforce this "hate" and all the anxiety you have about the social situation, every time you say you hate it. If we keep saying we hate it, we'll always have anxiety about doing it. We have made our negative self-fulfilling prophecy come true.

Instead, we must turn the tables on the ANTs. Your brain will hear and believe rational thoughts better than it believed negative and irrational thoughts. So, let's tell our brains the truth from now on – and turn our back on lying ANTs beliefs and feelings.

Your brain can be your best friend, if you use it in that way.

The Social Anxiety "Automatic" Cycle

Those of us with social anxieties are *too aware* of our nervousness and fears. It makes sense that we are too aware, because the anxiety and fear is happening to us, and we're the ones feeling it inside our bodies. Other people are not feeling your emotions; they are concerned with how *they* feel.

As a result of the strong internal anxiety we feel, we tend to be afraid that everyone else notices it and is aware of our fears, too.

It's almost like we feel other people are "psychics" at times, especially when we feel vulnerable and self-conscious.

When we think that "everyone is looking at us" or "everyone is noticing that we're weird," we add pressure to the situation.

Some of us have developed the idea that we're walking funny or strangely, or in some way different than what is "normal." We stop and look at ourselves in the mirror to see if we look strange or if we look normal. We train ourselves to watch our image everywhere we can – in mirrors, in store windows, in the glass in car doors, and even in rain puddles, because we feel there's something wrong with us.

If we feel there's something wrong with us, the conclusion we make is that everyone else sees there's something wrong with us and we remain self-conscious and continue to feel we're being watched and judged negatively.

Others of us have not been able to loosen up in public and may not be able to smile naturally. As a result of this always-present facial feature, we come to the conclusion that everyone can tell we're "fake," that we put on our smiles, because smiling and fitting in with the group doesn't come naturally to us.

Of course, think about this: maybe it's not coming naturally because you are putting too much stress and pressure on yourself to be "natural."

If I think others see me as being nervous, then I TRY not to be nervous because I don't want to be seen that way. I say to myself, "I've got to hide my anxiety. I don't want others to see I'm anxious or nervous. It's embarrassing, and causes even more anxiety."

Because I try to hide my anxiety, I put more pressure on myself.

The more we try not to be nervous, the more nervous we get. Sound familiar? This is another paradoxical part of life.

By using negative emotions, such as beating ourselves up, or trying not to be nervous, we add pressure to the situation… and then what happens? We become nervous, we sweat, we turn red, we feel afraid, our hands tremble, or our voice grows weak.

Why are these things happening? Because we've pressured ourselves strongly not to do these things. We don't want to look anxious to others – so we put more pressure on ourselves not to look anxious.

It seems like the right thing to do at the time… we don't want anyone to see our anxiety, and we don't want other's disapproval, so we do our best to hide our anxiety from others.

But this doesn't help. The solution to this symptom is counterintuitive and is another paradox, but this is the way the brain works.

The more you try to hide anxiety, the more you give it time to grow and expand. So, by trying to hide it by pressuring yourself, you are paying too much attention to your anxiety and making it stronger.

"The Social Anxiety Automatic Cycle" should remind us of the "Fighting Paradox" from an earlier session. The harder we try, the farther away from our goal we get.

If we keep on trying, worrying and pressuring ourselves about our perceived failures or about not being able to do everything that others do… by trying to hide our anxiety… we find ourselves trapped in that negative "automatic" cycle of fear.

Although this can be difficult to believe at first, think about and consider what I am about to say: Our fears and anxieties are nowhere near as apparent to other people as they are to us.

When we're feeling anxious, the anxiety is so bad that we somehow think other people must be able to notice and feel it, too. When other people are around and we're feeling anxious, we feel we need to hide it – like there's something everyone will see in us and it will make all of them dislike us.

In reality, we might be blowing our anxieties out of proportion to the actual danger involved.

Even though we feel anxious, other people may not notice it at all. We are very good at hiding our negative feelings. If I think people are noticing my anxiety, I get more worried and more anxious, and I try to be as "normal" as possible so that others won't see how weak and pathetic I am.

I am doing a number on myself, and adding even more pressure to the situation. I am sabotaging myself and my life by putting all this pressure on myself.

I need to relax, take it easy, and realize that maybe what I'm afraid of is not as scary as I once thought it was.

Most people with social anxiety have a very difficult time believing that other people are not noticing their anxiety, because the emotion of fear is so very strong, so personal, and so viscerally felt. "If I feel this anxious," they reason, "everyone else must notice I'm scared, too. How could they not?"

Keep in mind this may not be true. People may not actually be able to see inside you and see that you are experiencing anxiety. It may not show on your face, and even if there are physiological symptoms, most people don't seem to notice them, or they ascribe them to other causes.

Your head and stomach are not turning a different color, so how can others really tell that you're feeling anxious?

About the only way other people could know when we're feeling anxious is if we tell them.

Without the physical manifestations of anxiety, people can almost never tell how you're feeling, just like you can't tell how others are feeling inside just by looking at their face.

You may think you can tell, but their emotions are private. Only they are experiencing them. There is no way for you to know how someone else is truly feeling unless they tell you.

Your anxiety is not usually noticeable to other people, and that's actually part of our problem: no one believes we have social anxiety when we tell them, because we look and act normally. We look and act just like everyone else.

How You See Yourself and the World, Part I

Through your own personal perspective on life (that is, how you view yourself interacting with the world), you literally *create* the world around you. The world, as it exists around you, is put together or constructed by your own brain – and your world relates to how you currently see yourself.

The world is a construction of the human brain, and the reason people see the world in very similar ways is that we all have a human brain in our head that is structured to interpret things in the general way we do.

This is a very complex subject, so there's no need to get too scientific about it. People without social anxiety usually see the world more optimistically than we do. We view ourselves and the world around us more negatively or pessimistically.

Because of social anxiety, we see and interpret events from a negative point of view; not because we want to be negative, but because our brain has been conditioned and brainwashed into thinking this way.

Our negative bias tells us to be careful, to hesitate, to defend ourselves, and to keep ourselves safe from other people and situations. Our brain has been brainwashed and conditioned to avoid people and social situations.

We are more likely to expect negative things to happen, too.

For example, if you automatically expect others to like you, they usually will. If you automatically expect others to dislike you, they usually will.

You set up these expectations in your mind because of the beliefs you have about yourself, and then you automatically act on your beliefs, and make what you expect to happen... happen.

Let me re-state this:

What you believe about yourself comes true over time. Your brain makes you act according to what you believe. What you believe becomes your reality.

That last paragraph is very profound, so keep it in context. Read the paragraph over again and hold this statement in your mind as we move forward. Here are more examples:

If I believe that a certain situation, like meeting new people, causes me anxiety, then it does. If I believe that introducing myself to people in a meeting is scary, then it is. If I believe that giving a presentation in front of others is horrible and I hate doing it, then the thought of giving a presentation will cause me great amounts of anxiety.

Why? Because I've set myself up to believe that these situations cause anxiety. I'm prepared to feel anxious. I've told myself meeting new people brings on anxiety. So, when I meet new people, my brain causes me to feel anxious and afraid.

If an anxiety-provoking situation is mentioned or thought about, the result is that I feel anxious. My belief system has been developed and strengthened by what I've said and thought over many, many years.

What I believe about myself comes true.

Because I expect to feel anxiety, my brain is on the lookout for situations that cause me anxiety. The brain is on the lookout to make my self-fulfilling prophecy come true, and the brain fires and wires together to cause anxiety.

Let's stop here. Obviously, if our brain is in the habit of expecting the worst to happen, we have things to change. We'll need to act differently, so that our belief system changes and becomes more rational. That is where we're going with this discussion, but fully understanding the problem is a necessary first step to changing things.

If my brain believes that a situation – like meeting new people – always causes anxiety, then it unconsciously does its best to make this come true. The stronger my beliefs are, the more things happen in the way I expect them to happen.

What we believe at the start – influences our view of the entire world. If we start off with a negative bias, it's likely we see the world as an unfriendly place. As a result, we begin to believe that we don't fit in as well as other people.

Therefore, we feel uncomfortable around other people. This all started because of the negative, skewed way we see others and the world around us.

Let's move ahead with more examples. We need to grasp the importance of all this.

If you expect rejection, you tend to hide, avoid, stay silent, and be hesitant. Other people may interpret your behavior as a lack of interest on your part, or to the fact that you are "different" or weird.

If you expect to be liked, you will be outgoing, friendly, willing to take the initiative, and willing to talk and be open. As a result of the way you act, other people see you as a nice, friendly person.

The negative cycle you are in may have convinced you there is something wrong with YOU. That is not true. The only thing you may be doing wrong is viewing yourself and the world inaccurately.

The cognitive therapy we're doing is vital. We must start to RE-think our beliefs about ourselves and our lives.

Here's another profound statement: "What you give out – comes back." This is not meant to be new age, philosophical, or eastern mysticism. It is a rational statement, grounded in common sense. "What you give out – comes back." Let me explain.

If you are hesitant and indecisive around other people, they will react to your indecision and be hesitant with you, too. They sense there's something unusual about your actions, but they don't know exactly what it is, so they are reluctant to get too involved with you.

They can't see you have social anxiety – they just see you're hesitant and tentative.

Because of social anxiety, you censor yourself and give out indecision and hesitancy.

You're tentative and not quite sure what to say or how to act. Others respond to you by being hesitant and tentative in return. They can't see you have social anxiety, so they are reacting to the way you act.

What you "give out" to other people, comes back to you.

If you are too quiet, others may feel uncomfortable around you. Your silence makes you stand out from the crowd and you're viewed as "different," "timid," or "too reserved."

People usually feel more comfortable around others like themselves because it takes the guesswork out of social situations. Being quiet and timid doesn't help us make friends and influence other people.

If we hide from life and avoid social interaction, others will see us as unfriendly, "reticent" and as a loner.

People do not react negatively to us as individuals, they are reacting to the way we act or behave. We act the way we do because of our beliefs and feelings: in the way we have been "conditioned" to believe in the past.

Funny Stuff is Great Medicine Against Social Anxiety
Using Your Sense of Humor: Laugh, Smile, Lighten Up

Some good news for us is that recent research found that laughter stops the stress hormone, cortisol, from flowing freely throughout the body. When we laugh, there is a physical change in the body and brain, and this is a direct antidote to anxiety. Laughter is an anti-anxiety activity.

It's great to smile and laugh more often, and to be more open and light-hearted.

Laugh every day, as many times during the day as you can. You will feel a physical difference by laughing more. You can start laughing by yourself at home, and then gently bring this natural laughter out with time.

Smiling to yourself, when you're home alone, may be the way to begin. Smile and laugh more when you're alone to get into the habit of smiling and laughing more when you're in public.

You are not smiling to practice smiling. You are smiling to make you feel more light-hearted and less serious. With time, you will be able to take things less seriously and laugh in public as well.

The physical and mental benefits of laughing will add to all your other therapy strategies.

If you could bottle up laughter or synthesize it into a pill, the result would be a super drug capable of treating everything from anxiety and depression to heart disease and cancer.

Researchers have found that laughing is strong medicine that physically:

- Boosts the immune system.

- Triggers a flood of neurochemicals in the brain called "endorphins," which are the body's natural pleasure-inducing feeling.

- Lower the levels of cortisol in your body dramatically, due to an *increase* in the endorphin levels in your blood.

- Less cortisol leads to less anxiety.

There is a direct link to anxiety here. Laughter, or humor of any kind – cuts down the level of cortisol, which is the stress or fear hormone in our body – the one that tries to keep us stuck in our anxiety. "Laughing" directly changes things in your brain. It is more powerful than you or I realize.

Please see the online session material for additional added benefits of laughing, and using your sense of humor. Laughing Clubs exist throughout the world where the object is to come and laugh for the sake of laughing. You're literally practicing on laughing.

While it can be awkward at first, as you continue laughing, you relax, and laughing becomes a more natural thing for you to do. When you can access your laughter sooner, you can cut down your anxiety sooner. Laughter is a big anti-anxiety strategy.

Paying attention to comedies, and to anything you find humorous, allows you to lighten up and not take life so seriously.

IF YOU FIRMLY BELIEVE SOMETHING:
You Will Always Seek Out Evidence to Support your Current Beliefs

Your brain seeks out and twists the truth around until it finds evidence,
even if the evidence is weak and arbitrary,
to support what you already think and believe.
The brain is protective of your current belief system.
It does not want to change.

If you strongly believe something, you will always seek out evidence to confirm your existing beliefs... even if your strongly held beliefs are completely irrational, inaccurate, and false.

As examples, here are some strong "beliefs" that people with social anxiety have before they start group therapy. These statements come from people with social anxiety who were applying to participate in one of the groups at the Social Anxiety Institute:

1. I will never make any friends (or have any relationships). As soon as people find out more about me, they will not like me.

2. My anxiety is too strong. I have it in every situation. Everyone can see it and it's embarrassing. I always feel out of place and ashamed. I don't think I will ever fit in anywhere.

3. I am too anxious to take a job that has any additional social responsibilities. I can't discipline or fire people. It's just not in me to do that.

4. I hate it when other people notice me and put too much attention on me. Talking with one person isn't so bad, but when a group forms around me, and I am the center of attention, I feel like dying. I want to get out of that situation as fast as I can.

5. People do not like to be around me. I don't know what it is... I guess I give off the wrong "vibes," or maybe my eyes are doing something weird... I just know I am doing something strange and people notice it.

6. There is no hope for someone like me. I've never connected with anybody. I've had acquaintances, but never a good friend. What's wrong with me?

7. I avoid everything because of my anxiety.

8. I get so anxious because I don't know where to look. My eyes are always doing something and eye contact is very hard for me. Thinking about who to look at and for how long is stressful.

9. My hands shake when I eat at a restaurant or around other people. I'm afraid they'll see my hand trembling as I use my fork and spoon. Sometimes, my hand shakes when I'm picking up my glass and I know everyone is looking at me and judging me.

10. I sweat too much, and I can't hide it very well. Everyone can see my perspiration, even when no one else seems hot.

11. My face turns a bright red anytime I get mildly embarrassed, and everyone notices. I know they don't like it and they feel sorry for me. Any little thing makes me embarrassed and I blush.

12. I am disgusting and horrendous looking. How can anyone ever like me? I'm too ugly. How can anyone ever want to be seen in public with me? (This belief is called a "dysmorphia." Less than 1% of people with social anxiety are dysmorphic, but it is part of the social anxiety definition).

Notice all these strongly-held beliefs are false. None of them are rational. That is, they are not based on fact... in reality, they are inaccurate, irrational, pathological lies.

These irrational beliefs exist because whatever we believe grows stronger over time, and the brain automatically notices everything that agrees with its current belief system. The brain seeks out any corroborating evidence to reinforce its current beliefs, and discounts or rejects things that don't fit in.

Finding evidence to support its current beliefs is the default setting for the brain. In order to be stable enough to allow us to live, the brain has developed the habit of holding on to beliefs that it has believed for a long time.

For example, if you have social anxiety, the brain seeks out evidence to prove to you that you do indeed have social anxiety. You notice every little symptom of social anxiety and you beat yourself up for having it.

If you're anxious talking to one person, the brain picks up on it and tries to expand this out as far as it can. It is protecting itself and its current belief system. Our brain focuses on these symptoms, and tries to find evidence that supports its current beliefs about having this horrible nightmare called social anxiety.

The brain focused on the problem, instead of on the solution.

The brain doesn't want to change. It needs some direct encouragement from you. This explains why sometimes we don't want to go through days of depression, but our brain rebels at the idea of doing anything about it.

We know we can get up, get active, and do something constructive, and we will get out of our negative mood. But it's just so easy to sit there, think things over some more, and allow ourselves to wallow in the mud.

We know it's the wrong thing to do, but it feels right, because we've been doing it for so many years. The brain doesn't want to change – you need to gently nudge yourself forward.

The brain also rejects or discounts anything it doesn't currently believe. When I was given a compliment or some positive feedback from other people, I couldn't accept and believe it. I couldn't believe what they said because *it didn't agree with my current beliefs.* So, I discounted or rejected what the other person told me, and continued to cling to my own old beliefs.

How can we *change* the brain's habit of reinforcing what we already believe?

1. Sit down and consider that perhaps some of your beliefs are inaccurate. Write down two or three main beliefs about yourself that are irrational.

Question these old beliefs. Ask yourself, "Is this really accurate or have I been believing irrational things about myself for years?"

2. Relax, do not pressure yourself for an answer, and stop thinking about it by moving forward with your day and doing something constructive.

3. Tomorrow, look at your list again, and question your core beliefs. Are they really accurate? Tell your brain it has permission to discover what the truth really is.

4. **Pull down all the resistance, all the walls, all the defensive barriers you have erected to shield yourself from the truth. Are these defense mechanisms really needed?**

5. Are your core beliefs valid? Question this gently every day until your brain comes to a logical conclusion. Do it nicely and peaceably, without pressuring yourself. But don't just accept your old beliefs. Question your old beliefs and find out if there is really any truth to them.

6. If you firmly believe you need to be self-conscious, for example, decide to look around more and investigate whether or not people are noticing you and finding you to be a misfit. Is this belief accurate? Use the "look around technique" from an earlier session to do this, since you've already used this strategy before.

7. Having these thoughts as part of your belief system means that they are strongly-held beliefs. Once you start believing something, and it becomes a solid part of your belief system, it wants to stay alive (allegorically). Your brain is accustomed to sending signals down the same neural pathways. Your belief system has become a habit. It is habitual and that's why it happens automatically.

8. We are breaking up old entrenched *habits* of thinking in the brain as we gradually question our currently-held beliefs, reassess the evidence at hand, and begin to change our beliefs.

The Brain Recycles (and recycles) What We Already Believe

Your brain has many thoughts, beliefs, and emotions that may be incorrect and irrational.

These cognitive thoughts and beliefs, and the emotional content they carry, make you act and behave in ways you do not like – such as avoiding people and situations, being afraid to hang out with people, including friends and family, and going to class with other students.

The brain recycles what it knows. The irrational thoughts that form a habit seem accurate to you when your negative emotions seem to verify them. Thoughts carry emotions with them, but it is important to know that what you think and what you believe about yourself is what causes you to act negatively against yourself.

The more years that you recycle inaccurate ANTs filled garbage about yourself, the more it *feels* "right" and accurate to you. The more that it feels right and accurate, the more likely it is that you behave in a manner consistent with your beliefs. Even when the belief isn't rational and it isn't true, it still feels comfortable, because you've held the belief for a long time.

This is a vicious negative cycle that people with social anxiety are trapped in. You don't need to remain stuck in this negative recycle bin. Because of habit, the brain recycles your old belief system and the habits that go along with it. We must break out of this cycle by slightly changing how we think, act, and feel.

Because the brain believes what you tell it (within common sense), if you've said repeatedly that you can't make a friend, you can't make a friend. You predicted it and it came true. You made the decision that you can't make a friend; you believed it and made it happen. Your brain makes it happen by causing you to feel anxiety each time someone gets "too close" to you.

This goes even further. If you don't believe you can make a friend, you don't even *try* to make one. Your negative belief is so strong that you have given up. You feel hopeless and helpless. You feel that it doesn't do any good to try, because you've "known" for years that no matter what you do, you won't be able to make a friend.

This is a vicious habit of anxiety. You automatically respond to the idea of making a friend by saying "I can't do it. I've tried before and it doesn't work." Because you believe that, you make no attempt at making friends because you "know" it wouldn't do any good.

Habits are hard to break, so what's the solution?

The brain is malleable, or changeable. This "plasticity" means that literal changes in your brain are possible. It means that change is certain if you decide to change. If you think more rationally, you will act more rationally, and if you act more rationally, your feelings become more rational. *You* are in control of what you think, feel, and believe.

To un-learn old habits, we must teach our brains what they need to know. Our brains are not in charge of us, we are in charge of them. The brain changes with time, practice, and consistency.

All the handouts we've been doing up to this point reinforce rational ideas, beliefs, actions, and feelings.

You've taken the initiative and led your brain in rational directions, and reinforced rational thoughts. You guide the brain to recycle rational thoughts now. You are moving farther away from the irrational, negative habits that kept you stuck in social anxiety for such a long time.

Make this decision. Don't let your brain boss you around, like it did with me. Take charge, be proactive with life, and keep moving forward even when things seem hard. It is your consistency and persistence that allows the changes in your life.

The brain will recycle your new rational thoughts, feelings, and emotions. That's the good news. Let's keep the momentum going in this direction.

How You See Yourself and the World, Part II

For people to see us accurately, they need to see us for who we really are, and that means we need to make adjustments concerning what we do.

Staying silent and letting anxiety inhibit us is a recipe for disaster. If we want to change how we are perceived by others, then we have to change our behavior. We must do it one step a time, of course, but nevertheless *we* are the ones who need to change if we want people to see the real "you" inside.

The solution to the way people see us involves action on our part.

Here's what we need to do to change the way people see us:

1. Act a little friendlier, by saying "hello" or "good morning," make small talk, and open yourself up to talking a little longer with acquaintances and co-workers.

2. Be more open, by acknowledging other people instead of avoiding them. Wave at them or nod your head in greeting. In a meeting, you can nod your head in agreement with something being said by the person in charge.

3. If you're in a meeting or with a group of people, speak up every once in a while. This can sound scary at first, but let's use the "start with the easiest" situation rule. When you're not feeling too anxious, and you have something to say, or something valuable to contribute to the conversation, just speak it out. Sometimes we are ready to say something, but we hesitate and the moment passes us by. Instead of giving in to hesitation and censoring ourselves, let's stop the thinking... and start the doing.

4. If you have something to say, say it. Don't wait around. Just say it. You will feel better afterwards, and the other people in the meeting will have

heard you say something, and realize you're "there," you're a normal person, and you sound cooperative and friendly. You have "*inserted*" yourself into the meeting and are now a part of this group. The small comments you make can open up a whole new world of interaction with other people. The key is to relax and stay away from overthinking everything. Speak up, when appropriate, even if it's just a small comment. Don't hold back and censor yourself. Let other people hear your voice.

Hesitation is something to work against, since we overthink and overanalyze everything to death, and all our overthinking and overanalyzing makes us hesitate and censor ourselves.

Remember the phrase "*Stop the thinking… start the doing*" and it will help you move ahead instead of staying passive, sitting back, worrying about everything, and doing nothing.

5. When you make a change in your life, you will begin to receive different reactions and rational feedback.

How you see yourself and the world is what determines what your life will become. By making the small changes mentioned in this handout, you will see yourself in a different light, and this will calm you down and reduce your anxiety.

The way you see yourself is what you'll become. The brain takes what you strongly believe and makes it happen. If you're not seeing yourself and the world accurately now, then make sure to make the changes in your behavior that will let people see the real you behind the anxiety.

As you see yourself rationally and accurately, you guarantee that your brain will make happen what you want to happen.

Whatever you "set yourself up" for – happens.

If you expect to have friends, you'll act friendlier.

If you expect to overcome social anxiety, you'll continue making changes, and overcome social anxiety.

If you want to belong, to have meaningful friendships and relationships, then you will relax and stop worrying so much.

Your expectations about your life – come true.

There's always something you can *do* to change other people's misperceptions of who you are.

Now, does it make more sense when we say, "What you give out, comes back?" If you acknowledge other people, you are going to get positive feedback from them. They will never again think you're unfriendly, and they will always know you're open.

Keep this up, take one step at a time, and you will be carrying on enjoyable conversations with other people sooner than you think.

If you give out friendliness, you get friendliness back. If you are attentive to other people, they will be attentive to you. If you calmly carry on a conversation with them, they will calmly carry on ones with you, too. Slow down, slow talk, slow think, take your time, and take it easy.

What you give out, comes back.

After you've put these basic things into place in your life, you will feel better about yourself and you will feel better about the world around you. You have demonstrated you have control over your own life, and you have positive feedback to prove this to yourself.

You have acted on life instead of letting life act on you.

Once you feel more rational about things, avoidance and anxiety are no longer able to get in the way. You can view the world from a different perspective – honestly, accurately, and truthfully.

Maybe saying hello to people isn't the hardest thing to do for you anymore, and maybe now you can make acquaintances and friends, based on the fact that you can control and lessen your anxiety by using the strategies talked about in this session.

You are in the process of feeling comfortable around other people and fitting in – all because you acted and did something to change things.

You took the initiative and said hello to people first, acknowledged their presence, and were willing to make small talk with them. Because of what you did, people can see you for who you really are. They can see you honestly and accurately.

Whether we know it or not
We Are Always Doing "Therapy" on Ourselves

Here is a message from a young man using the original therapy series, "Overcoming Social Anxiety: Step by Step."

Hello all,

I just had a revelation last night while going over the ANTs handout, which I'd like to share with the rest of the mailing list.

Being a skeptic and a pessimist, I avoided doing therapy for a long time, thinking it was stupid and only worked for gullible people.

I thought repeating things to myself was basically telling myself lies so I could avoid reality and be happy. I thought I was too smart and that it wouldn't work for me.

But last night, I realized what power there is in repeating rational things to myself. I realized:

That's how I got this way in the first place!

I have social anxiety because of what I said to myself.

All it took was some critical teasing in grade school, and I got it into my head that I was awkward, and that I had nothing good to offer anyone.

As the years went by, and without ever realizing it, I repeated this to myself over and over again. Every goof up and every little mistake I made just *proved* that I was a worthless loser.

I thought I had too good a grip on reality to believe in rational reinforcement.

This is interesting because my "reality" had already been shaped through repetition and reinforcement of my negative thoughts and beliefs.

Now I see the power in telling yourself rational things.

Now I see the power of rationally talking to yourself.

It's a matter of perception, and perception is changed through repetition and reinforcement. We're all living proof of that.

Therapy is the same thing we've been doing to ourselves for all these years, except rational therapy takes anxiety away and makes us feel better, not worse.

For the first time in years, I feel like life will get better.

So to all you skeptics out there unsure about the therapy, try and look at it in a different light. **Reinforcement and repetition of what is rational will change the way you think and believe.**

Thanks for listening,

-- Todd

"I CAN'T DO IT" THINKING
Another Attack on Healing by the Lying ANTS

You believe you can't make new friends – because you've told yourself that for many years.

You believe you can't give a presentation – because you've beaten yourself up about your presentations for many years.

You believe you can never be assertive when you need to – because you've told yourself for many years that you can't handle confrontations or arguments with others.

Regardless of how you feel, you don't want to use the "I can't do this!" explanation. You are saying something strong and absolute – something you believe is true in *every* circumstance – and if your thinking is absolutely negative and irrational, this leads you to fully believe you can't *ever* do certain things because your anxiety is too high.

It is unnecessary to scare yourself like this.

You won't even *consider* doing some things because you've told yourself for many years that it is impossible.

You feel that some situations are too anxiety-provoking, so you just "can't do it."

This is nothing more than avoidance; the habit that's kept us locked into social anxiety all our lives.

Remember that your brain hears, believes, and responds to every word that you feed it.

Therefore, if you constantly say things like:

- "I **can't** make phone calls, I get too flustered!"
- "I **can't** go to the party, I won't know what to say!"
- "That meeting at work is **awful!** It sends my anxiety through the roof…"
- "I **hate** it when I have to meet new people. I feel so inadequate…"
- "I'll **never** be able to stand in front of a group of strangers without having massive amounts of fear!"

Your brain picks these statements up, and sure enough, you can't do these things because you've programmed it into your brain over and over again. You don't entertain the possibility of doing these things, because your brain believes you are not able to do them.

You've said these things so many times over the years that you have made something negative become reality. You have created your own self-fulfilling prophecies.

The brain believes what you say to yourself repeatedly. The more you reinforce the "cant's," "hates," "never's," and other forms of automatic negative thinking, the more time it will take to reinforce neutral and conditional language, so that the brain can be open to change.

Because your brain hears everything you say over time, you believe what you've said, regardless of whether it is rational or not.

What we decide to pay attention to makes a world of difference because it changes what is about to happen.

If your anxiety is on the rise, it's because you're thinking about it. You are expecting something bad to happen when you focus on your fears.

By focusing internally on your fears, you've opened the door for anxiety to attack.

- ➢ Anxiety has no power of its own. When I let it in, dwell on it, and analyze it, then I give it power.

- ➢ I will focus on external things, humorous experiences, or interesting conversations with other people.

> I will ignore anxiety because it is not based on actual fact. Anxiety is not dangerous. It's an irrational self-fulfilling prophecy.

> I will keep my brain open to the truth: Anxiety and the vicious cycle it traps me in is a blustering, bullying liar. It looks big and scary, but it is full of hot air. There is no basis in fact for any of its predicted outcomes.

Ultimately, you have the power to focus on anything you want. To overcome social anxiety, we focus externally and become interested in things we enjoy doing. Carrying through this therapy point and doing what we want to do, and at the same time enjoying it, is the essence of a proactive, happy life.

All that holds you back now is your belief system, particularly those beliefs that anxiety created and strengthened in the past.

These old beliefs are not true, so let me remind you that all solutions to anxiety are paradoxical in nature. To get over anxiety, we must do the opposite of what we normally expect to do.

Instead of fearing anxiety, laugh at it if you can. Call its bluff. It is there to scare you, but it has no power to do anything else. Begin to realize more fully that its days are numbered.

Stay focused ahead, and anxiety is dead

This may be a silly rhyme, but, nevertheless, it is true.

One theme of this handout is to stop absolute negative thinking like:

- I **can't** do it...
- This is **too** scary...
- I'll **never** be able to...
- I **can't** do that...
- It's **impossible** for me to make friends.
- I **hate** having to introduce myself at work or in class.

Instead of using absolute language, we turn the tables on the ANTs by going neutral.

Break up those absolute beliefs you have, and use conditional words, such as "Maybe I feel this way today, but things can change as I make progress. Maybe I can make friends. Maybe introducing myself to others is not the hardest thing in the world. Maybe I've made mountains out of molehills."

Now, let's combine turning the tables on the ANTs with paying external attention.

You believe you can't do certain things because they cause too much anxiety. Paying attention to external things does not give the brain time to think about anxiety and how awful it is.

Take a proactive stance and find something to focus on that will engage and interest you. Exercise, aerobicize, jog, do calisthenics, swim, use progressive muscle relaxation, read an interesting book, sing, or call a positive friend and talk about anything, except anxiety.

This is what we've done in this session: we've combined several therapy strategies into one comprehensive strategy to deal with social anxiety.

1. Stop the absolute negative thinking ("I *can't* do that").

2. Allow your brain to stay open to new ideas and alternative explanations. "Maybe you can do things after all."

3. Focus externally on other people and the world around you. Stay away from internal focusing and all its pitfalls: overthinking, overanalyzing, doubt, uncertainty, and fear.

4. Act on what you know is rational. Don't become a sitting duck, dumbly reclining on the sofa as the weight of your worries and fears consumes you.

5. Be proactive and engage yourself in life, interests, people, conversations, activities, and things you enjoy. If they're not right there in front of your eyes, hunt them up by using the internet. Search for the activity you're interested in and find other people who live near you that are interested in the same thing. Meet them, talk to them, and enjoy your new friends and activities.

Keep in mind that your brain hears everything you say and (eventually) believes it. Let's start believing rational things.

Beginning Behavioral Activities

You have some things going for you now that you didn't have in the past. Now, you can remember to:

- Calm yourself down as much as possible
- Loosen your muscles and relax
- Take one nice deep breath
- Use slow talk when talking to other people
- Focus externally on other people and listen to what they're saying
- Deliberately think slowly and take your time, so that your thoughts are better organized

Your conversations will go much more smoothly when you use these strategies you've learned.

Then, just keep putting these strategies into place in any situation where making a conversation is necessary; this is a daily thing for most of us. You'll find that the more you use these strategies, the stronger they become for you. They will also become automatic over time.

You won't need to remind yourself to loosen up and slow down for the rest of your life... as you do it repeatedly it becomes a habit.

The brain develops neural pathways making it into a new habit for you, and, you will automatically slow down and take it easy as you talk to other people.

But for now, calming down and loosening your muscles up, using slow talk – and remembering not to speed up – will keep your anxiety in check. If you don't speed up, if you use slow talk, then your body will not have the chance to send out excessive amounts of adrenaline and cortisol.

Use slow talk with this "easy" person in an "easy" situation to start the process of learning to feel comfortable about it.

If it causes no anxiety at all, that's fine. What is important here is that you are taking only one step, and are not causing yourself too much anxiety along the way.

By deciding to take the easiest route to start the strategy with, you will not have a setback; you'll feel more in control, and this enables you to move forward.

When you feel comfortable and non-anxious talking with easy people in easy situations, then move it up one step. Talk to another "easy" person, or talk for a longer length of time.

There are other people in this situation or you will be at another event soon, so choose someone else that you feel relatively comfortable around, and start the process again.

Suggestions for Putting Cognitive Therapy into Place
Doing Activities using Cognitive Strategies

Here are some suggestions for individual "experiments." You only need to start with one. As always, start with the easiest suggestion, or choose an activity of your own that seems more comfortable and has less anxiety associated with it.

When you have done this activity enough that you don't feel anxious about it anymore, pick another suggestion, and keep moving forward.

Pick one of these to start, and make sure you carry it through:

1. Choose something you liked while you were at a restaurant, such as the service, the food, or the atmosphere, and deliberately tell the waiter, manager, or owner that you were happy with their restaurant and/or service.

2. Borrow a small item from one of your neighbors at home or co-workers at work. It can be anything, but something inconsequential is best to start with (e.g., ask to borrow a stapler from a co-worker). Asking for help can be difficult for us, so any type of situation in which you ask for assistance makes a good experiment.

3. Ask a stranger for directions on how to get someplace you're going, even though you know perfectly well how to get there. The practice is in asking a stranger for help. Stay calm, use slow talk, and you'll find this may not be as scary as you once thought. Maybe it will be relatively easy. Because you took the initiative and were proactive, it may even make you feel better.

4. When you receive a call from a pesky salesperson at home, say "No thank you" and then hang up. Do not wait for their response and do not let them keep talking. As you grow stronger with this ability, just hang up the phone when a salesperson interrupts your day. It may sound harsh, but it is part of their job.

Don't be mean or angry; just be polite and firm. You don't need to waste your day on inconsiderate people, and you don't need to let them lay a guilt trip on you. You have done nothing wrong and there's no rational reason to feel guilty.

5. Say something positive about yourself to a friend or family member, in the context of what you're talking about. "I can do this" as opposed to "I could *never* do that…" Or, you can say "That's something I might like doing!" or "I've done that before and thought it was fun!"

6. An eye contact exercise:

    Make direct eye contact with a person on television… perhaps someone who is lecturing or reading the news to you.

    The next step forward would be to maintain short eye contact with people you meet at work, school, social events, or just walking down the street. A second or less of eye contact is quite normal in western societies, and one second is long enough. Practice this in a safe public area, and be aware of the possibility of physical attraction throwing this experiment off.

7. Call a friend or acquaintance – whoever is easiest for you – on the phone, just to say hello or to ask for something. For example, if you work together or are in the same class, you can ask for clarification as to what the professor or boss said about something.

    Our problem with phoning is that we think too much about it. So, from the very first experiment you do, *stop the thinking… and start the doing.* Just pick up your phone, punch in the number, and talk, without going through tedious, anxious amounts of time worrying about it beforehand.

    You have talked to people before, and you have talked on a phone before, so stop all the thinking and the worrying, and pick up the phone and call. You will be OK on this one. Thinking too much (overthinking and overanalyzing) is what *causes* anxiety. Talking on the telephone (doing it) decreases your anxiety.

There are many other individual behavioral exercises we could practice, and I imagine you have already thought of some of your own.

Setbacks:
Two Competing Neural Pathways in Your Brain

Setbacks happen to everyone as they recover from social anxiety. Unfortunately, I have never worked with anyone who didn't experience a few "setbacks" on the road to full recovery (it happened to me, too).

But please remember this – You can't have a setback unless you've already made some progress.

Let's put this in both physiological and neurological terms:

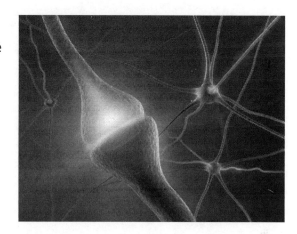

Your old neural pathways (the billions of nerve cells in the brain that transmit messages, thoughts, and emotions) automatically lead you toward your old responses: anxiety, fear, and depression.

This old pathway is tangible – it is real. It has now been mapped out in the brain by brain imaging equipment and the results have been published in leading scientific journals. Since your old neural pathway was used for many, many years, it is normal that the thoughts and beliefs that traveled along these pathways became ingrained, automatic habits.

However, when you began therapy, you also began to develop a new neural pathway system. You learned new ideas and strategies. You read things that may have been hard to believe, but were rational and logical. You used what you learned in your daily life, by putting the cognitive strategy into place with real people.

As a result, millions of brain cells began carrying the new messages you were learning: the methods, strategies, techniques, statements, and concepts that help us to overcome social anxiety. Your new neural pathway system was created and began growing.

The more you read everything over, and "sunk" the information down into your brain, the *stronger* you made this new neural pathway system. The more you continue to apply and use these new methods you are learning to real-life situations, the stronger your new neural pathway system becomes.

The more you use the new, and the less you use the old, you are literally changing the way your brain responds to events (automatically and habitually). That is how we get over anxiety – your brain starts to use the NEW neural pathways you are creating and reinforcing in the brain.

The brain operates in much the same way as the rest of the body. It operates under the "use it or lose it" principle.

→ **New Pathways Grow Stronger**

If you use your new, rational neural pathways, they grow stronger.

→ **Old Pathways Grow Weaker**

If you ignore the old anxiety pathways, they grow weaker.

We want to use what we know is best for us – to continue the changes in our neural pathway systems.

Currently, you have two competing neural pathway systems in your brain concerning anxiety. The old neural pathway is not entirely gone yet, so there is always the possibility that we might experience a "setback."

The worst kind of setback is after you've felt anxiety-free for a few days and anxiety seems to be under control. Naturally, you think you've got anxiety pretty much licked. Then – out of the clear blue sky – and without warning – boom! Something unexpected happens, and the old anxiety floods back in (pretty strongly), and you are left feeling defeated, hopeless, and doubting your progress.

You've had success in responding to anxiety with calmness and by slowing down already, but then some negative emotion is triggered, and your brain starts using the old neural pathway system again.

It's hard not to get down on yourself when setbacks like this happen, but rationally, you must realize that you are now one step closer to getting better.

You had a setback, but it's the amount of progress you've already made that allowed this setback to happen.

What actually happened is that through some old association or remembrance, your old neural pathway got stimulated, and the OLD consequence happened to you before you had time to stop it: you had anxiety – but this time it occurred when you didn't expect it to happen.

Let's look at the reality here:

This "setback" is actually a sign of progress. It is a good experience in the long run, not a bad one.

But, at the time, it doesn't feel like a good experience. It feels quite the opposite. It feels like all is lost and the therapy you've been doing has all been for nothing.

We know this is not really true, because as soon as you calm yourself down and get rational again, everything you've learned and done is still there in your brain. You haven't lost any ground at all.

The emotional negativity that anxiety causes can be strong and overwhelming. It has the temporary power to get under your skin and block your brain from seeing the rational truth. You get down and depressed and you feel like all hope is gone.

But that isn't really true. The moment you act against this negative emotional feeling, by calming and slowing yourself down, you will see that you can get rational again, and getting rational means you see the progress that you've made. You haven't forgotten any of the strategies you've already learned. You still remember how to slow yourself down, use slow talk, and take one step at a time whenever you're working on reducing anxiety in the real world. It's all still there.

The setback – the strong negative emotional pull that it created – made you feel hopeless, but the setback is not telling you the truth. The setback is an ANTs lie that can temporarily get you off track. If this happens, despite how you feel, get rational with yourself as soon as possible.

Your new neural pathway systems have not been damaged in any way. In fact, if you learn to handle the setback in a better way, you are strengthening your new neural pathway systems. We need to start viewing the entire process in this rational way.

Our old neural pathways somehow got stimulated or triggered, and our new neural pathways did not have enough time or strength to respond. Therefore, we had a setback.

If you begin to see what is really going on inside your brain, you start to respond by using your new thoughts, strategies and methods.

You must call anxiety's bluff – what really happened was a last ditch attempt at pulling you back into "anxiety-land" – to get you to believe that you haven't changed at all: that you are still totally hopeless, and that the therapy doesn't work for you, and that things will stay bad forever.

But, since you are developing that new neural pathway system in your brain, it is impossible for you to be pulled back to your old way of thinking permanently.

Your new brain pathways do not die out unless you totally give up, and even if you did that, it would take a long time for these pathways to fade. So, even if you have a setback, your new neural pathway system is still there and will continue to keep growing.

To save yourself emotional pain and feelings of depression, call anxiety's bluff as soon as you can.

Say to yourself:

"This setback feels terrible and I don't want to do anything but sit here and wallow in all the mud. But I know this is the wrong thing to do. I am going to get up and get active – I'll exercise, sing, talk to a positive friend, dance, play sports, or do anything so that my mood improves."

Don't Cling to Old Irrational Beliefs
Keep Your Brain Open to New Interpretations

We want to keep an open mind so that we can find out the truth about ourselves. Is there a rational basis for symptoms of social anxiety?

If what you find doesn't square with your current belief system, then you have evidence to support your reasons for believing differently.

Any time you notice a discrepancy between what you believe and what you are currently experiencing, then turn the tables on the ANTs.

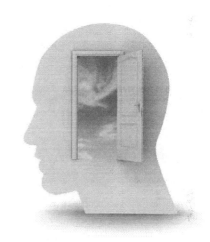

Talk to your brain every day and tell it the truth. Self-talk what is rational to yourself. You are a social anxiety detective, discovering what is actually true, clue by clue.

We can strongly believe that we do a terrible job of meeting new people, and that others dislike us as a result.

But, at the same time, you may be encountering contrary evidence to your old belief; evidence that disproves what you currently believe.

You may have noticed that people respond to you in positive ways or someone else might have made a comment about talking to you that was positive.

By default, your brain refuses to accept new evidence because it runs contrary to your old, strongly-held ANTs beliefs.

At present, your current (irrational) beliefs are too strong for you to accept or even perceive reality as it truly is. The world is entirely colored by the irrational, inaccurate beliefs you have about yourself.

Thus, you discount or reject all the evidence that runs counter to the old beliefs about yourself.

We do not want to keep doing this. A change is necessary and must be gently put into place.

You need to start considering that maybe you have an inaccurate picture of yourself and the world around you. Opening your mind up to see things more rationally and clearly is necessary.

Insistence on these old, strong, negative beliefs means that something is wrong. ALL the warning lights are blinking.

The more you insist and refuse to consider alternative explanations, the more you continue to believe your strong negative beliefs. All the resistance that you're putting up makes it more likely that it is YOU who are viewing yourself and the world inaccurately.

Use self-talk and say to yourself every day:

- "I want to find out the truth. I don't want to have a closed mind."
- "I open my mind up to any and all information concerning my anxiety. I will consider anything reasonable."
- "Maybe my old thoughts and beliefs are wrong. I don't know."

"But I'm not going to reject new ideas and explanations anymore. I'm going to keep an open mind."

Believing inaccurate things about ourselves holds us back for years, and ruins our life in the present day. Instead of meekly accepting your old beliefs, question them gently (are they really accurate?) and open up your mind and test things out.

Find out what is rational, regardless of what you currently believe. If you suspect your perspective is somewhat warped, then test it out. Do not keep accepting a long held belief without questioning it.

Many of our strongest beliefs are the most irrational and inaccurate of them all.

The brain has terrific power. We can use it to help us get better, or we can use it to keep on believing inaccurate, irrational lies.

Please consider this carefully and move in a healthy and helpful direction. Test things out and be rational. Open your mind up to the possibility you MIGHT have been wrong in your past assessments. At least, maybe that could be true.

Stay open to finding out the truth, and be rational with yourself. If you do these things on a daily basis, your brain will gradually become more rational, given some time and patience.

How You See Yourself and the World, Part III
Your Belief System Runs and Rules Your Life

The story I am about to relate is a true story in all the basic details. The time was one hundred years ago, before the advent of radio and television, and before the residents of this Caribbean village had electricity and running water.

Henri was born into this small village on the island nation of Haiti, where his mother taught him from a very early age the culture, art, and religion of voodoo.

Henri sat in the circles when religious chants and ceremonies were being held. He heard the blessings and the curses made by the shamans and voodoo priestesses.

And Henri saw with his own eyes that when the religious leader made a prophetic announcement, it was accepted as the truth by everyone. There was no arguing, debating, or disagreeing with the shaman.

As Henri grew up, his belief system grew stronger and stronger. Henri became more and more convinced that what he was being taught was true. It was part of his daily life. It was part of his daily conversation. He lived with these thoughts and beliefs every moment of the day and night.

Everyone he knew believed them. No one challenged them. It did not occur to Henri that there could be anything different.

As a young man, Henri believed everything he was taught because he never saw or heard that there was anything different. His belief system was never challenged, and he never heard of people having alternative thoughts, beliefs, or ways of living.

To him, the shaman's words always came true. He believed it because he had seen it happen over and over again with his own two eyes. Whatever the shaman said came true. The shaman was always right.

Henri's belief system concerning voodoo was very strong. Whenever beliefs are as strong as this, the brain closes itself off to any new ideas, and notices only things that reinforce its current belief system. With a strong belief system, this makes what you believe come true.

Henri saw and believed, and his convictions grew stronger over time. He reinforced his belief system by going to the ceremonies, talking to his family, and conversing with his friends who also believed. When he was old enough, he went through the rites of passage to become a man. This tied him even more closely to his family, friends, and other villagers.

Everything Henri did and said *reinforced his belief* in the power of voodoo. To Henri, it *was* the truth.

Westerners have always had a hard time understanding the "voodoo curse" because it doesn't seem logical and we have no situations similar to it.

Back in Henri's day, when shamans put a "death curse" on an enemy, the curse caused people to fear for their lives so strongly that many fell dead of fright.

When victims have been cursed by the shaman in a public religious ceremony, and they believe strongly in the power of voodoo, life becomes an agitated, terrifying wait for the inevitable doom that is to occur: their death.

When an autopsy is performed on the person who was cursed, no logical reason is found for the death. The person is usually young, vital and healthy. He can be healthy and fine one day – and be dead the next. Is this the power of voodoo at work?

If not, what is the cause of death? What doctors found when they autopsied the bodies of people who died from being cursed, was that they had died because of fear! Henri literally scared himself to death.

When you're cursed by the shaman, and you believe in his powers, the adrenaline and cortisol levels in your body hit the roof. Adrenaline and cortisol flood the body to such a degree that the excessive stress causes a massive heart attack. During an autopsy, adrenaline and cortisol can be found almost everywhere throughout the body.

Where did this fear come from? A strong belief! But was this fear rational? No.

It was a strong false belief, but it was a belief that Henri internalized. He believed that whatever the shaman said would come true.

The power of our beliefs is stronger than anyone realizes. There are many other true stories like this throughout human civilization and culture.

Belief is a very powerful thing. We live our lives based on our beliefs, and we live inside the "reality" they create for us.

Therefore, it is important for us to develop beliefs that are rational, healthy, strong, positive, and life enhancing.

A strong belief always has a powerful effect. When you learn to turn the tables on the ANTs so that you can begin believing the truth, your life begins to change; your beliefs about yourself and the world come true.

So slow yourself down and become rational. Get away from emotional reasoning. You have to believe what's reasonable, so this means using self-talk to reinforce what make sense.

Talking to yourself out loud and telling your brain what is rational begins to change your belief system by changing your beliefs.

As your belief system changes and becomes more rational, you start to gradually make life changes. Your thoughts and beliefs are changing, and, as a result, you begin thinking more rationally.

Behavioral Activities, Part II

Here are some additional behavioral exercises that you can begin doing by yourself, without a group, right where you are.

Please do not push too fast or try something that brings on too much anxiety. But please do take one step at a time and *do* these exercises. You don't get better unless you are acting against anxiety. You need to combine the cognitive strategies you learned with a situation in real life that causes you anxiety, in order to make progress.

Add these suggestions to the last list and work on one, two, or several behavioral therapy activities every day. You might start off with a small experiment you know you need to work on. Although we're starting out small, your steps add up quickly, and you always make faster progress than you think.

1. Call a governmental (city, state, province, federal) number on the telephone, and when someone answers, ask if you can speak to Mrs. Demingson (or any other obscure name you want). When you are told there is no Mrs. Demingson in the office, or that you have the wrong number, say "thank you" or "I'm sorry" and hang up.

That was really no big deal – people call offices all the time and need to talk to a specific person. When you ask for Mrs. Demingson, most of the time they'll just tell you no one by that name works there. If you reach someone who is nasty or abrupt with you, remember they are probably in a bad mood, and you don't need to internalize their negativity.

So what if someone hangs up on you? That is a normal thing to do sometimes and it shouldn't be taken personally. The people on the other end of the line don't even know you. So, don't take things personally or blow them out of proportion. Just laugh, accept it, and move on.

2. When you're at work, in class, or at a social gathering, look for people who are new and alone, and make it a habit to introduce yourself first, and start a friendly conversation with them. Make sure you can do this within the context of the situation. The other person will be grateful to you for taking the initiative and making them feel less out of place.

3. Start a conversation with a stranger at the grocery store that is limited to questions about the food and food products you're buying. (In context, you can do this at any type of store). For example, you could be reading a label and ask a passer-by for assistance in reading the ingredients. Or maybe there are new vegetables or fruits in the produce section, and you can ask another shopper what they are or what they taste like.

4. Smile, establish one second of eye contact, and say "hello" to a stranger as you walk by them in public. Just continue walking on. If you can't smile, then just glance at them, say "Hello" or "How's it going?" and see what kind of response you get from them.

5. While you're in your car, turn on the radio or put in your mp3 player and sing along to songs that you know. Particularly, sing when you are stopped at a traffic light and another car is beside you. To get started, you might want to sing a little and hum while you're traveling and keep quiet when you're at a traffic stop.

*All of us are in a different place in putting these strategies into place in our own lives, so you need to modify the experiment so that you're doing the easiest experiment first, and working your way up to the ones that seem harder. **Make sure to use the "Look Around Technique" with this one, too. You may be surprised that not too many people are paying attention to you.**

6. When you are driving outside of your own neighborhood, wave at a stranger in their yard – like you know them. See what their response is.

7. Return something you purchased from a store. This should be something that doesn't work or doesn't fit. Instead of avoiding the situation and taking the loss,

go ahead and return the item to the store. Notice that you feel better about yourself after you have done this.

8. Make it a point to wave at and acknowledge your neighbors *first* when you see them outside. Take the initiative in being friendly. This is the beginning step of showing friendliness to other people. When you are feeling more comfortable, talk briefly with one of your neighbors, and gradually increase the number of neighbors you talk to and spend time talking with. Choose the easiest person to start with and keep moving it up. If you do this every day, you've made a lot of progress in a week's time. Keep it up, because you'll be in a much better place in a month.

9. Go to a bookstore, find the section of books that you enjoy, and see if there is a person there reading a book. If so, ask them a question about the book or the subject matter, even if you know the answer already. You'll find that most people respond pleasantly and, by being open, the potential is there for to have many positive small talk conversations.

10. Invite a friend over for a meal.

11. Give a compliment to someone when it is deserved.

It is a good idea to list these suggestions on a piece of paper. You choose the behavioral assignments for the day, and remember to do them. They should be organized, and you should do something on the list at least every day. Start with the easiest situations, and keep repeating and reinforcing them until you feel comfortable doing them.

Because of individual differences, there are many additional behavioral activities I haven't suggested to you that you may want or need to do. **Anything that causes self-consciousness or makes you fear being put on the spot is a behavioral activity to work on.** Do these experiments with the therapeutic approach we've been using, and you will be fine.

It will be necessary for you to add your own behavioral activities to this list. I am staying very general with the suggestions. But each one of you will have specific behavioral experiments that are relevant to your own life, which you want to work on. Keep a list of the behavioral experiments you're working on, and check to make sure you're doing them every day.

From a therapeutic or "getting better" point of view, the **main thing is that you are *doing* the experiments.** It's good that we've been talking about them and that you understand them, but now you have to *do* something about it. You have to act on what you know so that you can make progress.

Learning the cognitive strategies is necessary, but it won't help you at all until you use the cognitive strategies in **regular daily situations.**

Get going with this and don't let anything hold you back. Even if you have a bad day, relax, and realize that *everyone* has bad days. You certainly do not need to beat yourself up over it.

Try several of these behavioral experiments, modify them to fit your own life, and keep working at them **systematically** until the anxiety about that particular situation is gone. When the anxiety is gone, move up to another experiment that causes you a little anxiety and repeat it until the anxiety goes away.

Stay in the present moment as much as you can, use the look around technique, and calmly let your brain process everything that is going on around you.

No overthinking or overanalyzing. There is always a behavioral experiment you can do in any situation, so start slowly and move up from there.

STOP THE THINKING – START THE DOING.

Active Listening, External Focusing, and Taking the Initiative

Active Listening

Active listening means I am going to pay attention to what other people are saying. In the past I went inside my head, worried about what I was going to say, and felt anxious. Now, I am going to do something different. I am going to listen actively to the other person, shifting my attention to an external object.

One thing social anxiety does to us is try to hog the spotlight and keep us focused on our fears. Anxiety loves being the center of attention and tries to keep you paying attention to it. Anxiety wants you to go inside your head and worry.

You won't have the time to put active listening into place if you allow anxiety to keep you worried.

Instead, let's turn our full attention to listening to the other person.

We would all be better off if we listened more. Sometimes those of us with social anxiety feel like we're already good listeners because that's what we've done most of our lives. The reason we don't talk as much as others is because talking about ourselves causes us anxiety.

The fear of talking is not a good reason for being an inattentive listener. To get better, we want to focus our attention on the other person, and listen to what they are saying. If we listen to other people, then our old internal thoughts will not be paid attention to.

So I focus on another person and actively listen to what they're saying to me.

Let me take this one step further and emphasize the word "active" in front of listener, and you'll get what I'm saying. By *actively* listening to others, I am choosing to focus on them, understand what they are saying better, and respond to them logically when it's my turn to talk.

If I'm actively listening to other people, I won't have time to go internal and focus on my ANTs thoughts. Instead, I'll focus on listening to the other person, and I'll be able to remember what they're saying.

All we need to do is think about "active listening," and then, when you're talking to someone else, in person or on the phone, listen to people more attentively than you usually do. Attune your brain so that you place more focus on what others are saying. This will reduce your level of anxiety because you are no longer paying attention to it; you are paying external attention to the person you're listening to.

This doesn't mean you stay quiet and just listen to other people; quite the opposite. **If you are actively listening, you will have more to say when it's your turn to talk, because you'll remember more of what the other person is saying.**

Active listening cuts down on anxiety and lets you focus on the other person, so that you can have longer conversations as time goes by and feel more comfortable doing it. As you focus on the conversation, it will go smoother than it has in the past, and nothing awkward will happen.

By focusing on the conversation, you'll have the right words to say and all your conversations will be easier. As you stay calm and refuse to be rushed, your feelings of anxiety will go down.

Active listening makes the other person the center of attention, and anxiety cannot hog the spotlight by making you focus internally on your fears and worries. Attentively listening to other people reduces your anxiety and frees you up to talk comfortably with other people.

External Focusing

The second strategy is paying external attention to other people.

We already know that focusing internally on our own anxious thoughts and feelings reinforces our problems and makes anxiety stronger. Therefore, we need to focus externally, away from ourselves and toward the situation or other person.

Paying attention to our inner feelings (or internal focusing) always spells trouble for us and leads to anxiety. We have been paying internal attention to anxiety all our lives. Anxiety likes to be the center of our attention, so paying attention to our anxiety just leads us to have more of it.

Instead, I decide to spend my time listening to and focusing *externally* on others, talking to them, and learning to enjoy their company. I always have something to say in conversations because I have been actively listening and know where the conversation is going. If I'm focusing externally, I don't have the time or energy to make my social anxiety the center of attention.

These two methods take practice, but, like everything else, it's a process that gets easier with practice. Don't expect to become a global conversationalist in just a few weeks. Work on these methods a little bit at a time, until you find yourself automatically listening and paying external attention to others.

Taking the Initiative

The third thing we need to do is to act first, or to take the initiative, rather than always responding passively to things that happen to us. By taking the initiative and being an active player in life's events, we feel better about ourselves, our self-esteem rises, and our confidence goes up.

This is another paradox, but paradoxes contain solutions to puzzles. Taking the initiative may seem that it would cause you more anxiety, but in actual fact it does the opposite. When you take the initiative by acting first, it takes the pressure and stress off you and does not allow you to feel strange or awkward.

This may not seem logical at first, but as you start taking the initiative, you discover that your anxiety goes down and you feel better about yourself.

If you take the initiative and act first then you will feel less anxious and more confident. You are proactively engaging with the world and the people in it.

Now, you are an active participant in your own life.

When we hide and avoid and respond *passively* to life, we feel more bottled up and inhibited. The more "inactive" we are, the more anxiety and depression we feel.

The more we act on life, the more control over our beliefs and emotions we'll have. Taking the initiative in social situations *boosts our confidence* and *decreases our anxiety*.

You have some control now over your anxiety, whether you know it or not. You have acted on life instead of giving up and reacting passively to everything that's thrown your way.

Let me give you an example:

Let's say you take the initiative and volunteer to help with a special project at work. You make a choice, take the initiative, and join a group of other people. You made yourself an active player in life. This cuts down your anxiety, and allows you more social contact with other people.

Other common ways you can take the initiative are:
- Volunteering
- Exchanging personal greetings before the start of a meeting
- Talking to another person first
- Approaching others to welcome them to your job, city, or social group
- Answering back any calls or texts you received on your phone when you weren't available

There are many different situations in which you can take the initiative. Pick the easiest situation and do it. Use the look around technique to gauge how you are being perceived. Is anyone noticing you? Does the person you're talking to seem grateful that you chose to talk to them? Or are there hate groups all around you, carrying signs with your picture on it, who condemn you for talking to other people?

The more we listen to other people **"actively" by focusing externally on them**, the more we will hear them correctly, the better we will be able to converse with them, and the easier our conversations will go. If we listen better, we will speak better.

If we take the initiative, say hello first, and start small conversations first, we will feel more in control, feel better about ourselves, and feel more confident and open. The more we feel confident, in charge, and open, the less that anxiety is going to have any power over us.

Active Listening… External Focusing… Taking the Initiative…

All of them have the power to lessen and reduce our anxiety. All of them have the power to make us feel better about ourselves.

VICIOUS CIRCLES AND HOW TO SHRINK THEM

Anxiety is a multiplicity of interlocking vicious circles. One problem exists inside another problem, and all our anxieties are interconnected members of each other. Anxiety is a tangled mess and tries to mess up your life in the same way. Once you get trapped inside the vicious circle, it is difficult to get out.

Thankfully, we don't have to worry about each individual association and all their inter-connections because by doing the cognitive therapy, and putting it into place, you and your brain will solve all the messy, confounding problems that anxiety causes.

Your rational brain will not allow itself to stay messy and keep things out of place. Your brain is ready to straighten everything out and put it in its proper order.

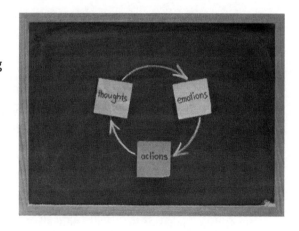

Let's do a short review here to keep us on track:

Fear and anxiety *cause* more fear and anxiety.

Calmness and relaxation cause us to be able to feel more calmness and relaxation. Whatever you focus on and practice, becomes stronger. **I decide to focus on calmness and peace because I know that will help me get better.**

Anticipatory anxiety is not only unpleasant, but it *causes* the worst to happen. Expecting the worst to happen makes the worst happen. Fear and anxiety push us in to the vicious circle, hold us in place, and inhibit us from taking the initiative whenever they can.

The vicious circle grows as we pay attention to it, focus on it, and dwell on any of its problems.

When we pay attention to it, when we dwell on it, when we focus on it, the vicious circle only becomes stronger, more powerful, and dominates our lives. The problems anxiety causes seem overwhelming and insurmountable because we're looking at it from anxiety's perspective.

Anxiety looks overwhelming because it puffs itself up and hopes you'll see it as a bigger problem than it really is.

Anxiety lies to you by telling you to quit doing the therapy because it doesn't work right away. Anxiety builds up negative emotions, beliefs, and expectations. We won't let that happen. We want to make certain that we're moving forward.

When we go along with anxiety and its vicious circle, we are giving it power, fueling it, and reinforcing it. We help it to grow. As we focus externally, relax, learn to take it easy and slow our thinking down, we are focused on the solutions, and the solutions begin to occur.

Your brain is ready to keep you moving forward if you just ask it to, and you give it permission to stay open and rational with your assessments and judgments. Keeping your mind open to other ideas and interpretations allows your brain to find the rational solution that answers all of anxiety's questions.

You and your own brain cooperate together in overcoming social anxiety. The brain is actually cooperating with itself. If you expect to get better and make anxiety a thing of the past, then this is exactly what will happen. The brain makes any rational expectation happen as you keep gently working on the cognitive strategies and putting them into place in your life.

What you expect to happen – happens. So let's make sure we have rational expectations and our expectations are in harmony with what we want from life.

It is rational to want to feel better when talking to an authority figure. Once I've rationalized the situation in my mind, and realized this person is no different than anyone else, I can put this rational belief into place.

I believe that I am just as good as anyone else, so I am entitled to talk to the boss or my supervisor without having feelings of dread. It is illogical to have these feelings.

So to get them to go away, we move up our expectations and align them with what is rational. It is rational to talk to the boss when needed, so I need to do it without anxiety, dread, or fear.

You need to rationalize this with yourself first, and remind yourself that you are putting people on pedestals and building them to incredible heights, just because you feel they are better in some way than you.

Your irrational voice tells you that because they are better than you, they won't be interested in talking to you. Therefore, you expect to do poorly if you're forced to talk to them. It's easier just to avoid situations if our expectations are negative.

But these are irrational ideas and you have drawn an irrational conclusion. Once we think this through and come to a rational conclusion, then we can make a rational decision:

"I need to talk to the boss about this project, so I will. There's no rational reason to be fearful or anxious. I will expect what is rational – that I can talk to the boss and do OK.

The boss will like me better after I make myself known to her, and this will keep it the situation positive."

After rational consideration, I've decided there's no legitimate reason to avoid the boss.

I **expect** that when I talk to her things will go fine. I will **take it easy, relax, and use slow talk** to stay calm. I will not let adrenaline and cortisol get in the way. The boss will like it that I showed initiative and it will reinforce to her that I am interested in my job. There are only positive results that can come from this.

My rational decision led to a rational expectation, which led me to talk to the boss, and allowed me to do it without anxiety. It's actually no big deal. **I expected to be accepted even before I approached her.**

Maybe by approaching life in this way, many of the circumstances in my life will change. I have decided not to avoid everything anymore. I have decided I will have rational expectations. I have decided that my rational expectations will help me act in accordance with my rational beliefs.

The less we play the vicious circle's games, the better, quicker, and easier it will be to overcome social anxiety.

Decide what you will believe.
Calm yourself down, and expect the rational to happen.
Move forward, keep an open mind, and allow your expectations to come true.

Your brain takes in and believes everything you say to it repeatedly, and your brain is changing now. Your thoughts, beliefs, and expectations will become more rational as you allow your brain to find out the truth.

MINGLING

When you attend a social gathering, go into it with a realistic expectation, and be as rational as you can be with yourself.

Loosen up your muscles, relax, take a nice deep breath, and calm yourself down. Remind yourself to slow down and take your time before you talk with other people in the room.

Keep in mind it takes at least two people to talk. You are not responsible for "silences" and there is absolutely nothing awkward or wrong with quietness.

In fact, sometimes you feel most comfortable around people you know well, and silences are frequent and common. It's not silences that are the problem. It's what you think about them, and how you react to them.

We mingle with other people all the time. Sometimes, it's official, as when we mingle during a business convention or at a social gathering. Sometimes we mingle with people we already know, like we do at work parties or social get-togethers.

Here are some general therapy concepts we can start to use the next time we mingle with other people:

1. **If you feel you've run out of things to say, you can politely end the conversation.** Take the initiative, and say "I'm glad I met you, Mike. Please excuse me, but I see a friend that I need to go meet" or… "I need to get something to drink" or "I need to go outside for a few minutes" or "I need to make a restroom visit." It could be anything that is legitimate to the situation. You do not need an excuse to end a conversation – you are just following social convention and being considerate.

This is not a difficult thing to do after you've done it once. If you are done talking with a person, be polite and end the conversation. This is exactly what everyone else does, and you do not need to stand around and wait for the other person to act first. Take the initiative yourself, say "see you later," and move on. Walk over to someone else or another part of the room.

2. **Invite someone else into the conversation that is standing or sitting alone.** If you take the initiative to do this, it will make *you* feel better and reduce your own anxiety. Or, start a conversation with someone you can see is alone and has no one to talk to. Take the initiative and talk to them first. You will feel in control when you do this and this cuts down on nervousness and anxiety.

3. **You *never* have a legitimate reason to feel uncomfortable, ashamed, or guilty.** These are ANTs feelings. Reject them by labeling them as "liars" and *decide* to feel OK regardless. This may sound strange to you at first, but you can decide you will no longer feel uncomfortable or anxious at this point. The way to gently move forward and away from anxiety is to take the initiative and decide that there's no rational reason to feel uncomfortable or ashamed. You deliberately decide to feel OK instead.

   The brain needs to hear that you are no longer going to feel uncomfortable for no rational reason, and it needs to hear it repeatedly, so that your belief system can change. You have made a rational decision. Now, reinforce it every opportunity you get.

4. **Decide ahead of time that you *won't* allow yourself to be uncomfortable.** After all, why should you feel out of place? There is no legitimate, rational reason for this, so why do you need to let it happen? The pull of the past is there, but you can decide not to go along with it. You do not need to feel strange, awkward, or out of place. Instead, you should rationally feel OK because you belong in this situation and you are part of this group.

5. **You can stand in one spot all alone if you want and simply look around the room.** That is not against the law. You will not die because of this, and there is nothing rationally wrong with this. You are entitled to do whatever you reasonably want in these social situations. So stay in them, and refuse those feelings of being uncomfortable and not fitting in. Use the "Attitudes" handout to bolster your rational thinking...

SO WHAT?
WHO CARES?
WHY am I making a mountain out of a molehill?
THIS IS NO BIG DEAL!
I belong here just as much as anyone else.
I deserve to feel comfortable here and I am reinforcing this to my brain.

Then, take a nice deep breath, take any pressure or stress away from yourself, and relax.

It's not rational to feel uncomfortable in a place that you've been invited to or where you belong. You have every right to feel as good as anyone else. So, allow yourself to feel OK. Allow yourself to take in the rational truth and realize you do not need to accept the present that anxiety gives you.

You can accept your own present, and this present is the ability to feel calm and peaceful in this situation. It wouldn't be rational to feel any other way, and you have control over your own emotions.

So decide to feel comfortable, and you will be. Relax, and allow yourself to be comfortable. What you give out to others, comes back to you.

6. **Focus on other people** – actively listen and pay external attention to them – and note their names, interests, jobs, and what they are talking about in conversation. If you forget to do this, don't beat yourself up. Just continue forward. Remind yourself to do this, and the next time you'll remember.

7. **Slow your speed down as you talk**. You will almost always have something to say if you calm down and do not speed up. Here's where all the practicing you've done in slow talk pays off.

Now you can use calming talk in social situations where you feel anxiety, and the process of slowing down will change your emotions. When you remember to use slow talk, it calms you down, helps you remember, and organizes your thoughts.

Remember: The reason not to speed up is so you can prevent the excessive release of the hormones adrenaline and cortisol from speeding you up and stressing you out. You are in control of this now. By calming down and using slow talk, you can be in control of your emotions whenever you want.

I have had a few people throughout the years ignore slow talk and refuse to practice and use it. But there always comes a time when they realize that they made a big mistake by abandoning this strategy before it had time to work. If it's practiced and used enough, it has profound effects on your life, your conversations with other people, and your career choices.

8. **Those of us with social anxiety usually have years of experiences that we've never talked about or shared with other people because we always felt too much anxiety talking to other people.** Realistically, we have a lot of things to say to others!

    Remember you're conversing with someone else and you do not have to be interesting, witty, or funny. You do not need to be entertaining. Just pay attention to the conversation and engage in it. If you do that, everything else will take care of itself.

9. **You have the ability to mingle just as well as anyone else.** Turn the tables on your anxious thoughts.

    For example, say to yourself: "*You know, I used to think I couldn't mingle and talk with others very well. But now I realize I might be better at this than I once thought...*"

10. **Decide again that you will not be uncomfortable in this situation.** There is no rational reason for you to let yourself feel this way. Whether you're in a group or whether you're alone, you do not need to feel out of place. Take one nice deep breath and relax. Loosen your muscles with progressive muscle relaxation. Take it easy on yourself. It's OK. People are not focusing on you anyway. So just take it easy. It's no big deal – go with the flow and relax.

11. **You can walk through a room of people who are conversing and not talk to anyone.** Try doing this. Why should you feel self-conscious about walking through the room? Others do it all the time and don't think anything about it. Decide you're going to feel OK about doing this. There's nothing 'wrong,' strange, or weird about it. It will not make you the center of attention.

Prove this out to yourself by using the look around technique as you walk through the room. No one notices or judges you -- because they're all busy paying attention and talking to other people. Everybody else walks around the room when they want to. Go ahead, and prove it out to yourself. See what is rational in this situation. Give yourself permission to relax, slow down, and walk around wherever you want. Take the initiative, test it out, and you'll find it's no big deal.

12. **Switch people or groups politely whenever you want.** You are not "chained permanently" to the first person you talk to. Everyone moves around during a mingling session and talks to other people. Take the initiative, talk to people, and politely move on whenever you feel like it.

13. **Don't hang around the same person all evening.** You think you need a "safety" person with you, and maybe you did before you started therapy. But now you've made progress and you may not need that "safe" person with you all the time anymore.

Go ahead, move away from the safety person, and talk to other people. If it is still important to "step by step" this, then you and your safety person can move together from group to group to start with. When you feel more calm and comfortable, however, split up. Rationally, you are safe in any of these mingling environments.

Remind yourself that all you're doing is paying attention to the conversation and participating in it. You may have avoided these situations in the past, so give yourself some rational credit for engaging in conversation now.

14. **People who are talking with each other split up all the time.** It is an accepted (almost "demanded") part of mingling. You talk with someone for a while, and then you move on. No big deal. You can say the same things to the next person. They haven't heard what you've said prior to their conversation.

15. **Politely move on when you want.** Go to the refreshment table. If you don't see anyone to talk to, drink and eat. Go to the restroom. Take a walk around the room or go outside for a few minutes. Take it easy on yourself. This is no big deal for heaven's sake!

In another hour, all this will have faded in everyone's memory. People mingle to have fun and get to know each other. Don't take it so seriously. Be nicer to yourself, relax, and let go of any tenseness in your muscles. It's no big deal.

16. **No one is watching and judging your performance.** They have better things to do than to focus on you.

17. **Everyone is paying attention to themselves and their own conversations.** They want to enjoy themselves and have a nice time. Maybe you should do the same thing.

18. **Decide ahead of time that you're OK,** no matter what you do, what you say, or what happens. What you decide and what you expect can have major implications down the road. Keep in mind that if you're rational, your brain is going to follow what you decide. It will act on what you say.

19. **Your decision to mingle is a success in and of itself.** It is a success just because you did it. It needs no outside validation from anyone. You do not need to feel "great" afterwards. It was your decision to mingle – even if it is for a short period of time to start with. Making a decision, and carrying out your decision, is what counts. When you make small talk with someone, you are acting against social anxiety and being rational with yourself.

20. **By moving ahead like this, you gradually prove to yourself that you do fine when people are mingling together.** There is never any failure unless you give up completely and retire to the closet in your bedroom and never come out. Mingling was a success because you did it. You are in the process of being able to talk to other people without having anxiety.

This is just another small step in learning to live life without social anxiety. Keep moving forward step by step, take the initiative, make small decisions, and stay rational. You are doing fine. In truth, you have made more progress than you realize.

THE DESERVING STATEMENTS

Before you can comfortably express your own needs, you must believe you have a legitimate right to have those needs. From a rational perspective, you already deserve the following rights, whether you *feel* like it yet or not:

1. **I have the right to decide how to lead my life.** This includes pursuing my own goals and dreams and establishing my own priorities.

2. **I have the right to my own values, beliefs, opinions, and emotions** – and the right to respect myself for them, no matter what other people think of me.

3. **I do not need to *justify* or over-explain my actions or feelings to others.** Over explaining is a sign that I am not comfortable with myself and I feel a need to come up with excuses as to why I acted the way I did. I do not have to justify my actions. (Common sense guidelines here).

4. **I have the right to tell others how I wish to be treated.**

5. **I have the right to express myself** and to say "No," "I don't know," or "I don't understand."

6. **I have the right to take the time I need to formulate my ideas before expressing them.**

7. **I have the right to ask for information or help** – without having negative feelings about my needs.

8. **I have the right to change my mind.**

9. **I have the right to make mistakes as I learn new things.**

10. **I have the right to like myself even though I'm not perfect.**

11. **I have the right to have positive, satisfying relationships within which I feel comfortable and free to express myself honestly** – and the right to change or end relationships if they don't meet my needs.

12. **I have the right to change, enhance, or develop my life in any way I decide.**

When you don't believe you have these rights – you react very passively to events in your life.

When you allow the needs, opinions, and judgments of *others* to become more important than your *own*, you are likely to feel hurt, anxious, and angry.

Being passive and inhibited – by reacting to everything in life -- leads to further inhibition. Being passive is indirect, emotionally dishonest, and self-denying. Passivity keeps anxiety alive, and contributes to our low self-esteem.

Whether you believe "The Deserving Statements" right now or not is not important. We are on the way toward thinking about their meaning, and starting to believe what is healthy and rational.

"The Deserving Statements" can be the truth for us, as we gently consider all the options each statement implies. **Each "Deserving Statement" is logical and rational. Every human being has a right to feel this way.**

Perfectionism and Pressure:
Two Negative Emotions I Don't Need

I don't need to be perfect. I won't expect that of myself any longer. No one can be perfect, and besides, there is no "perfect" way of doing anything anyway.

If I'm not doing something as well as I'd like, I will rationally and calmly accept it.

But by trying harder and pressuring myself to do more things in a precise and inflexible way, I only make myself more miserable, and I will actually hurt my performance.

Free yourself from perfectionism and pressure

I will do what I need to do, but realize there is no perfect way to do it. I accept this calmly even if I have anxiety or if I don't understand something. There is no need to be perfect. Striving to be perfect only adds pressure. I won't expect that of myself any longer.

There is pressure in a situation if I put it on myself. Nothing is that important. It's all small stuff. If other people disapprove of something I do or say – who cares? People always disagree with others.

There is no pressure anymore because I no longer allow it. There is no one right way to do things. There is no pressure because there is nothing I have to do "precisely perfectly" in any given situation.

I can do whatever I want. I can accept it if someone judges me to be nervous. Therefore, there is no pressure, because I have accepted their judgment. There is no need to be perfect – no precise way to do things. Since there is not a precise way to do things, there is no pressure.

There is no pressure because I can do whatever I want. There is nothing I must do. There is no exact right thing to do. There is no pressure because I can handle the consequences of my actions.

There is no pressure because other people's opinions do not determine how I feel about myself – or whether I am a worthy human being. There is no pressure because I don't have to be perfect... I won't expect that of myself any longer.

I put a great deal of pressure on myself when I analyze every situation for the perfect way to do it.

But, I remember: Analysis = paralysis.

When I feel pressured, I'll stop the thinking and start the doing. There is no universally perfect way of doing anything, so whatever I do will be acceptable.

If after doing something, I think I could have done a better job, I'm just going to say to myself, "Well, I learned something here, and this knowledge will help me do a better job next time. It's OK. I don't need to be perfect. I am satisfied with my efforts."

My self-esteem is not determined by how I perform at a certain task – or whether others judge me as being intelligent, competent, interesting, or good-looking.
There is no pressure because I accept it when someone judges me to be anxious. If someone judges me as a failure in a certain regard, I accept this too, because I don't need their approval to sustain my self-esteem.

My opinion concerning the value of my work is more important than the opinion of other people.

My belief about whether my attitude is good is more important than anyone else's.

My comfort with how I carry myself and what I do is more important than anyone else's.

And there is no pressure because as a human being I have the right not to justify what I do to others.

Even when the "perfectionism" monster hits, this doesn't mean that I am less valuable as a person, or that I should feel ashamed. I have more progress to make but I will keep using the methods I am learning now with cool, calm, confident, peaceful determination. I will do things for my own enjoyment and growth, and not just for the approval of other people.

Thus, there is no pressure, because if other people look down on my performance, looks, or the way I conduct myself, I can still be happy because I am doing things for my own personal satisfaction, not for other people. **I have the right as a human being to say, "I don't know," "This is not my area of expertise," or simply "no."**

I'm avoiding words like "should," "must," "can't," and "have to," because they make situations very rigid and stressful. I will do whatever makes me happy, from a rational perspective.

The more I try to pressure myself into doing a perfect job, the more problems I cause for myself, and paradoxically, the more my performance suffers.

External Focusing:
How it Keeps us Away From Anxiety

When we feel anxious in any way – and this includes anticipatory anxiety – we want our attention and our FOCUS to be on external things, not on our internal feelings.

Our internal feelings are not accurate when we're anxious, and if we pay attention to our anxiety, our anxiety grows stronger. Paying "internal" attention to our fears is what we've been doing all our lives, and it's a habit that keeps anxiety in control.

If we do the wrong thing and focus on the way we feel inside – we only reinforce and re-invigorate our anxiety. For example, when we

- Give a performance,
- Introduce ourselves to a stranger,
- Make a public presentation, or
- Do anything in public,

We do not want to notice how we're feeling.

Instead, we want to pay attention and focus externally on the things in front of us. Other people. The room we're in. The décor we see. Anything that is external. Focusing on the external things around us makes it easier to deal with what is presently happening.

Say to yourself:

> "I need to call my anxiety what it is – a liar– then I will focus my attention away from it. I will focus externally on something outside myself. I do not need to sit, dwell, ruminate, and scare myself to death by paying attention to irrational anxiety.

➤ I need to get active and get my mind moving in a positive direction, thinking about or planning some external situation or event."

We're following a logical progression as we get better, so what we pay attention to should be outside ourselves. Our focus should be on external situations and events.

We don't want to get into the habit of "checking in" with our anxiety, and then acting on the basis of how we feel. Feelings can be more irrational than thoughts, and negative feelings, like anxiety, love it when they trap us into paying attention to them. Our feelings lie to us, and if we focus on them, they will grow stronger and make us more anxious.

➤ I don't need to pay attention to my anxiety. I never need to be "checking in" with how I feel. I need to pay attention to things outside myself. I need to externally focus on other people, other situations, other jobs, other activities.

➤ My focus needs to be on something outside myself. Inside is where all the worry, doubt and fear exist, and where the ANTs like to trap me by getting me to over-think and over-analyze everything.

➤ I need to focus externally. My focus should not be on myself and the way I feel. My focus should be on other people and what I do.

We can never accurately gauge our progress by checking with the emotion that gives us pain, because if we purposely notice how much anxiety we feel, we end up reinforcing it, and allowing it to grow bigger. Focusing internally on our anxiety *is* the problem, and we're looking for solutions.

I need to ask myself:

Did I do what I needed to do?
Did I keep my attention external?
Was I focused externally on something or someone else?
Can I pay attention to the good, the better, and the beautiful?
Can I pay attention to the positive or nice things around me?
Can I calmly think to myself and remind myself to focus on external factors?

If I talked to Angela today, the question is "Did I pay attention to what Angela was saying, or was I thinking about how much better she is at making conversations than I am?"

Paying external attention and actively doing something is the solution to anxiety.

Pay attention to other people, external events, and the jobs in front of you.

"I'll never go back to overthinking and overanalyzing, because I know that analysis equals paralysis. Paying attention to things outside myself is my ticket out of anxiety- land."

Here are some additional examples of how focusing externally can help us:

You may feel exhausted because you've felt anxious all day. You may feel like going to bed because you are so tired. Social anxiety stresses us out and depletes our body of its natural and beneficial neurotransmitters after a few hours around other people.

We are mentally fatigued because of the heightened self-consciousness we feel. We're not fatigued because we did anything physically demanding. Notice there's a difference between mental fatigue and physical fatigue.

If you challenge this social anxiety fatigue a little, knowing it's irrational, you can nudge yourself to get physically active, move around, exercise, or go to an event that someone invites you to. The exhaustion that social anxiety causes fades quickly, and you begin feeling more upbeat and alive in a matter of minutes.

What happened?

Your internal feelings lied to you. You weren't as exhausted as you felt. The mental anxiety was making you feel physically tired and exhausted. By staying active and doing something regardless, you prove to yourself that the ANTs feelings are wrong.

Paying internal attention to your feelings is a trap.
Paying external attention to life around you is a solution.

When you get up out of your chair and actually go someplace with another person, you feel less tired rather than more tired. You nudged yourself to go out and, by paying external attention to things around you, you feel alert and alive. **We can move past this internal feeling of exhaustion by paying external attention and nudging ourselves outward.**

- Focusing internally on all my worries and fears makes my anxiety stronger and cycles me back into anxiety-land. Continuing to focus internally only keeps my problems alive.

- The solution to anxiety is to focus away from negative feelings and actively *do* something external. Focus externally on other people or other situations. I need to be as active as I can.

- I will focus outwardly and externally – not on the way I am feeling inside – not on the lying ANTs feelings and thoughts.

- Fear feeds on fear, but it can only do this when I focus on it.

- **So, I will do the opposite: focus externally, and actively listen to other people.**

How to Be More Assertive
Specific Assertiveness Statements

1. **Be as specific and clear as possible about what you want, think, and feel.** The following statements are clear and direct:

- "I want to..."
- "I don't want you to..."
- "Would you..?"
- "I liked it when you did that."
- "I have a different opinion. I think that..."
- "I have mixed reactions. I agree with these aspects for these reasons, but I am concerned about these aspects for these reasons."

It can be helpful to explain exactly what you mean and exactly what you don't mean, such as "I don't want to break up over this issue, but I'd like to talk it through and see if we can prevent it from happening again."

2. **Be direct.** Deliver your message to the person for whom it is intended. If you want to tell Emily something, tell Emily; do not tell everyone except Emily; do not tell a group, of which Emily happens to be a member.

3. **"Own" your message.** Acknowledge that your message comes from your frame of reference, your conception of good vs. bad or right vs. wrong. It is your perception. You can acknowledge ownership with personalized ("I") statements such as:

"I don't agree with you" (as compared to "You're wrong"), or
"I'd like you to mow the lawn" (as compared to "You really should mow the lawn, you know").

Blaming someone only makes them resentful and angry. Instead, frame your words in a personal, yet positive, way.

4. **Ask for a response.** "Am I being clear? Does this make sense? How do you see this situation? What do you want to do about it?" Asking for feedback can encourage others to correct any misperceptions you may have, as well as help others realize that you are expressing an opinion or desire rather than making a demand. Encourage others to be clear, direct, and specific in their feedback to you.

Learning to Become More Assertive

As you learn to become more assertive, remember to use your assertive "skills" selectively. It is not just what you say to someone verbally, but also how you communicate nonverbally with voice tone, gestures, eye contact, facial expression and posture that will influence others. *It takes time and practice, as well as being able to accept yourself as you make mistakes, to reach the place where you can be rational and act assertively.*

What Assertiveness Will Not Do

Asserting yourself will not necessarily guarantee you happiness or fair treatment by others; it won't solve all your social anxiety problems, nor will it make all your personal problems disappear. Just because you assert yourself does not mean you will always get what you want, but you have increased your chances tremendously. You are being rational, telling your brain the truth, and doing it calmly and without excessive emotion.

Lack of assertiveness is one reason why problems are never resolved. Inaction (i.e., doing nothing about it) fuels the fire of social anxiety and keeps it alive.

Let's work toward being more open, direct, and honest. We need to care less about other people's approval and more about what we think about things. By being assertive, other people will actually like you better and have more respect for you and your ideas. People like it when you stand up for what is rightfully yours in a rational, calm, non-aggressive manner.

How to Be Calm and Assertive:
An Example

If someone is picking on you, harassing you, or refusing to consider your ideas and opinions:

Be proactive about it. Acknowledge the problem. Don't ignore it and think the problem will go away on its own, because it won't. You can calmly meet the challenge by being assertive.

"I need to act on life instead of letting life act on me."

Aggressiveness, on the other hand, is the opposite of assertiveness. Aggressiveness involves anger, fighting, revenge, and pay back. Aggressiveness is a negative emotion that involves anger, and it has no part in overcoming social anxiety.

We are not going to play the game anxiety wants us to play – by using aggression – because aggression feeds and fuels our anxiety and makes our problems worse.

Assertiveness and aggressiveness are two very different emotions.

Assertiveness means you stand up for yourself when you need to, in a calm manner, without anger.

By using calmness and peace, you signal to the other person that you are serious about what you're saying, but you are not trying to knock them down or cause them harm in return.

If someone is taking advantage of you, this is a situation that needs to be resolved, and the only way it can be resolved is through being assertive. Over-emotionality, especially the use of negative emotions like anger, only muddies up the situation and puts us farther away from what we want. We become assertive when we think rationally and remain calm.

A person who takes advantage of you is not usually expecting you to stand up for yourself.

They think you're going to lie down and accept whatever they dish out. The next best thing for them is that you respond to their bullying by using anger.

Anger signals to them that they got under your skin and bothered you. Anger demonstrates to them that *they* have control over your emotions.

You've seen big childhood bullies take advantage of children younger and smaller than themselves. If children being bullied remain silent, they lose, and if they get upset, angry, and cry, they lose, too.

Neither
(a) ignoring the problem, or
(b) responding to it with anger
are answers to this problem.

A bully would love to get into an argument with you, so they can abuse you more, by letting other people see your frenzied, angry attempts at winning the argument, while they sit back, remain calm, and laugh at you. We are not going to fall into this trap.

The bully uses aggressiveness to get his way. We are not doing that. We are not using our negative emotions. We stand up for ourselves by stating our case calmly, and matter-of-factly. It's best to do it in a laid back way and without any hint of hostility.

The bully is not expecting you to be calm and respond in this manner. A calm, clear, rational response will turn the situation around and put you in control of it.

By being assertive you say,
"I've don't appreciate it when you do that..." (keep it factual)
"It seems like you get a big charge out of that. Why is it so funny to you?"
"I want you to call me by this name."

Be honest, direct, and to the point. You are addressing the issue that caused you problems in a serious manner. By remaining calm, and using slow talk, you get your point across more effectively.

The calmer you sound, the more in control of the situation you sound. Your voice will carry authority with it because you are staying calm and being precise in your wording. By being polite, serious, and reasonable, you will sound like the adult in the room.

So, if someone is picking on you, "riding" you, harassing you, or refusing to consider your ideas:

Ask them slowly, politely, and in a regular tone of voice … (using calm, slow talk):

"Why are you acting this way?" or
"You know, I get the impression that you don't like my ideas" or
"You know, you seem to be all worked up and upset over this" or
"What is it that bothers you so much about it (or about me)?"

Each situation is different, so change the wording to fit your individual circumstances.

Stay clear and rational, and speak to other person in a clear, calm tone of voice.

Calmness implies you're using slow talk and paying external attention to the situation.

By talking in a calming voice, the other person will listen to you, because you sound authoritative, serious-minded, and professional.

If the bully tries to use anger or aggressiveness against you, other people will side with the person who sounds calm and rational. It doesn't take long for other people to see who's right in these situations. Get your point across directly to the other person, but do it in a calm, slow-talk way.

As long as you are reasonable, the situation will work out in your favor. **Being assertive, and speaking up when circumstances warrant it, turns these situations upside down.**

By taking action, you will be seen as an active participant in life. You will be in control of how you see yourself and your life, and others will view you in a similar way.

To summarize, approach the situation calmly, keep your tone of voice low, and speak up. **Use slow talk to stay calm and sound authoritative.**

Reducing Self-Consciousness

When you have been using the look-around technique for several weeks, and have proven to yourself that you can loosen up and relax in public situations, there are additional ways you can build on this strategy and make it even stronger.

Here are some additional experiments we can do to reduce our self-consciousness:

1. **Deliberately clear your voice in a room full of people.** It doesn't have to be loud. You just need to be heard.

    Look around gently and see what the response is. Is everyone looking at you? Are people looking at you with a mean look on their faces? Are people looking at you with pitying looks on their faces? Or has no one noticed anything at all? Could that possibly mean that clearing your voice in public is not something you need to feel self-conscious about?

    By clearing your voice in a crowded room, and then observing peoples' responses, you will likely find that no one is really noticing you at all. This will allow you to discover the truth about what's happening, and will help lower your self-consciousness and feelings of inhibition. Test it out for yourself.

2. **Speak a little louder than you usually do, when the situation is appropriate.** Just by speaking a little louder, you cause your breath to be drawn from your diaphragm, which calms and slows your body down physiologically, and reduces your heart rate and blood pressure.

    What kind of reaction did people have when you spoke a little louder than you usually do? Did you see horror on other people's faces or did you get negative feedback from them? Did anyone cry out, "Hush! You're hurting my ear drums!" Were people visibly turned off by your louder voice, and did they run away screaming from you?

It's more likely that people paid more attention to you and listened to what you said. Did they seem more positive and attentive to what you said?

Just because you spoke a little louder than usual, do you need to feel self-conscious about it? What is the rational thing to believe? What should I expect the next time I raise my voice slightly?

If you noticed a positive reaction from people, then raising your voice a little is something you'll want to continue to do.

Most of us need to learn to be louder, so work on speaking loudly enough so that you can be heard. You are not taking tiny gasps of air from your lungs. You are breathing deeply so that you have more air to use for your voice.

I doubt people hate you because you're speaking loud enough to be heard. Think about this rationally, and then practice on being a little louder when you talk, like in the checkout line in a store, or when you have an appointment and are talking to the receptionist.

People like it when they can hear you and they don't have to keep asking "What?" or "What did you say?" or "I'm sorry. I couldn't hear you."

3. **Talk for a longer period of time to people that you already know.** Anxiety wants to hurry you up and rush you to get done, so that you stop talking, and get out of the situation as soon as possible – anxiety wants you to *avoid*.

   Instead of doing that, let's take our time, refuse to let anxiety rush us, use slow talk when necessary, and stick with the conversation a little longer. Prove to yourself that you have plenty to say, and you don't have a rational need to run away and avoid the situation. Slow down, relax, and take it easy. Stay in the present moment just a little longer.

4. **Go out of your way to welcome a new person at work or in a group.**

    Take the initiative and say hello to them first. See how they respond. Do they hate you for coming over and talking to them or are they appreciative that you took the initiative and talked to them first? What is actually true? Take one step, try it, and find out. Prove it for yourself. Most people like it when others greet them and talk to them. Most people dislike it if you stay quiet, silent, and never say anything to them.

5. **Sit in a slightly different way than you usually do.** Cross your legs differently, or sit less upright and rigidly than usual. Try loosening up and sitting in a relaxed manner.

6. **Feel free to stretch your body and yawn when it is appropriate.**

    If you stretch and loosen your muscles in public, will this feel better to you or will people give you negative looks and tell you to stop doing that? What will actually happen if you loosen up and sit in a more relaxed way? Test this and find out. See what stretching your muscles out does. You might find it relaxes you and is something that everyone else already does.

All of these behavioral exercises have the power to lower your self-consciousness and inhibitions, as you test things out in all sorts of different social circumstances.

By doing these activities every day, you will soon prove to yourself that others are not really noticing you or judging you to the extent you think they are.

Your self-consciousness will go down as you look around and notice these things. It is another counter-intuitive realization. By doing the opposite of what you expect, you find the solution to excessive self-consciousness.

BRAINWASHING

How do people develop anxiety disorders?

The simple answer is that they are literally brainwashed over time by other people and/or environmental circumstances.

When you hear negative comments, criticisms, and statements about yourself over and over again – over the course of many, many years – your brain begins to believe all the negative things that it hears.

If you are exposed repeatedly to brainwashing, your mind begins to think and believe what you've heard.

You've been brainwashed (or conditioned) into having an anxiety disorder.

The good news is that since you can be brainwashed into having an anxiety disorder, you can learn to wash your brain of it, too. Washing your brain of anxiety involves becoming rational with ourselves.

No longer are we going to be brainwashed. Through active, structured therapy, we are going to wash the brain of all the old garbage from the past, all of the old negative emotions, embarrassments, fear, humiliation, low self-esteem, depression, negative beliefs, and hurtful events.

You are going to brainwash in a rational way. You will replace these old irrational lies with new, clean, rational thoughts and feelings.

Washing the brain is more powerful than brainwashing, because washing the brain makes our thoughts and beliefs more rational. They are no longer warped in a negative direction.

When the old brainwashing thoughts come, talk to them.

Say to yourself:

> "This may be an old thought that was brainwashed into me when I was younger... but now I choose to wash my brain of it.
>
> I choose to act and think rationally.
>
> I choose to cleanse my brain of the old lies, and fill it with accuracy, truth, and rationality.
>
> I will not allow old brainwashing thoughts/feelings to continue to hold power over me. Instead, I deliberately choose to think and believe differently.
>
> I choose to wash my brain of the past and discover a rational way forward."

If we can be brainwashed into having automatic negative thoughts and beliefs, we can also wash our brains to become more rational. By becoming more rational, it will open up a whole new way of thinking for us. One incremental change at a time is important.

It's when you use your self-talk to wash your brain that it becomes an automatic event with a little time.

Give your brain permission to catch your irrational beliefs that were brainwashed into you. Allow the brain to replace the brainwashed belief with a rational belief instead.

The positive emotions we're using to get better – calmness, peace, relaxation, acceptance, and peace – already reside inside your brain, and the therapy we're doing allows these positive emotions to grow and take over.

THE PROFOUND CONCEPT

One of the most profound concepts in life is this:

**When you act (or do something) first,
your feelings (emotions) follow along behind.**

If you wait around to feel good before you do something, you'll be waiting around forever.

You take action first, and repeat and reinforce this action, and, as a result, your feelings and emotions change. Actions first, feelings second. It may seem backwards, but this is the way the brain works.

It would be nice if it was the other way around. It seems better for us to learn cognitive strategies first, reinforce them until they become automatic, and then feel our anxiety go down so that we can act on them.

Unfortunately, the brain doesn't work like that. The solution to anxiety is paradoxical, remember. First, you do what you need to do. Afterwards, your feelings change and your anxiety goes down.

The solution to the paradox is that we need to act on anxiety first before our feelings and emotions change. That means there is always a lapse in time between putting the strategies you are learning into place, and your resulting feelings.

**Feelings don't change unless you act first.
Action comes first, and then feelings follow.**

This is another reason we have been emphasizing taking one small step at a time. By taking one small step against anxiety, you can begin to feel better faster because you are doing something that will reduce your anxiety. By taking that one small step and doing something, we feel better more quickly.

You act against anxiety; therefore your feelings begin to change.

Keep on acting against social anxiety and your feelings continue to change. They continue to lessen and disappear. If you act against social anxiety, you will feel more relaxed, comfortable, and calm.

Taking action creates new feelings. Feeling comfortable, calm, and peaceful are positive emotions that occur. There is also a sense of accomplishment you feel after acting on what you know is rational to do.

Small steps are acted on and the brain knows you're taking action against anxiety.

If you take a step every day by exposing yourself to small anxiety-provoking situations, then the positive feelings will gradually follow.

Anxiety is reduced only after you act against it. Take the rational step first, and your feelings start to change.

Contrary to popular thought, action comes before the desired result.

If social anxiety makes you avoid things, then take one step against avoidance by going someplace new or doing something new, even if it is for a short period of time.

You have chosen something new to do; you have done something and acted against anxiety. Your brain will process what you did, and you will feel less anxious about it. The key point is you don't feel less anxious until you've acted against your anxiety first.

The more you act against anxiety, the more your feelings will change, and you will gradually feel less anxious when doing this new activity or going to this new place.

You won't feel better until you act first, and your feelings are a direct result of your actions.

Our anti-anxiety steps must be systematic and done in a "step-at-a-time" manner. The change in feeling occurs in the same way – a little change at a time.

"You will gradually feel less and less anxious" is the right way to put it, rather than "tomorrow you won't be anxious at all."

Anxiety goes away only when you ACT against it. It may take patience and time, but if you continue to act against it, your feelings will change. This is another guarantee we have because of the way the brain works.

Because you persistently do something to decrease anxiety, you are making permanent changes in the brain's neural pathway systems. When you've practiced enough, your new neural pathway system will begin to take over. This is scientific and has been proven to happen. As you change and do things differently, your brain changes, too.

MAKING CONVERSATIONS

In a social situation, pay attention to the person you are talking with and what they are saying. Focus your attention externally so that you can't be focused on internal ANTs thinking.

As you actively listen to the other person, notice they are:
- Making a statement
- Expressing an opinion
- Telling a story (such as something that happened to them)
- Talking about the future or future plans

Respond to what they are saying by:
- Commenting on their statement
- Giving your opinion of what they were giving an opinion on
- Asking follow-up questions to stories to clarify what they mean, and get more deeply involved
- Questioning their plans: What they are going to do? How far along are they in their development? What is their ultimate goal?

Try doing the same thing. If you know someone well, talk about something you're both interested in, or talk about something general that happened in the news, or an event that happened in your own life during the past few days.

When you feel you are stuck, ask the other person a question. This will cause them to start talking. Pay external attention and actively listen to what they have to say, so that you can make a comment or talk about something related in your own life.

Something another person said may have reminded you about something that happened to you. Don't hesitate. Open your mouth and talk about it.

Despite your old ANTs beliefs, people like it when you're open and you share things with them. They do not like it when you stay closed off and remain a silent listener.

A conversation is a two-way street. You talk, they talk. That is the essence of a conversation; two or more people sharing things about their lives.

It's a simple conversation that you can control by using slow talk. It's no big deal. People regard you more highly when you open up and share things with them, just as they share things with you.

Start talking about anything you like. Don't limit yourself. You can talk about anything reasonable. It could be something topical that everyone else is talking about, or it could be an interest of yours. It might be something happening in your city, country, or the world.

It's fine to talk about your interests, even if the other person doesn't share them. The only way you find out what people are interested in is if you open your mouth and start talking. You don't want to censor yourself all the time – this is a social anxiety habit we've been trapped in before, but now we realize that continually censoring ourselves leads us to be silent, inhibited, and avoidant.

Just open your mouth and say something and you will be OK. Stop the incessant thinking and start the talking.

It's something most of us have done to some extent in our lives anyway. Just don't be afraid to talk. Open your mouth, get ready to speak calmly, and your brain will start to work.

You have plenty of things to talk about, so when it's appropriate, open your mouth and TALK.

Once you do that, the brain will engage. **Getting started is usually the biggest hurdle, so calmly talk when it's reasonable to do so.** Once you get started, you'll feel better about yourself. After all, it's no big deal.

Everyone makes conversations, and you will receive subtle positive feedback from the people you're talking to. Someone may nod their head affirmatively, while others may open their eyes wider and listen intently. You can tell when you're being listened to.

Saying something adds you into the conversation; it puts you there, and re-affirms to everyone that you are a participating member of the group. This, in turn, reduces your anxiety and shrinks your fears.

Feel free to change the subject when it appears to have run out. For example:

"So, what do you think of…"
or
"I never thought it would stop raining last night…"
or
"I hope I studied enough for this test coming up…"
or
"I've heard this class is very interesting…"

To be a friend, you have to show interest in other people. The only way others can gauge that you are interested is by what you say (and in what tone of voice you say it). **Act interested, say something, and you will come across well to others.** From their perspective, you are a calm, friendly individual.

Should We Be Living in a Hostile World?

If we are afraid of looking foolish, fitting in, or being judged and evaluated by others,

If we anticipate upcoming events with a high degree of worry,

If we don't think we can hide our anxiety, thus making us more anxious,

If we are so self-conscious we wear ourselves out with worry,

If our anticipatory anxiety is so strong that we dread future interactions,

Then it's likely that we feel we're living in a "hostile world" where everything is set up against us, and we just don't fit in.

The initial reaction to living in a hostile world is to avoid. We stay silent and don't participate in life. When we talk, we do so hesitantly. We're constantly afraid of what's going to happen next. We've developed the habit of expecting the worst to happen.

Most of us with social anxiety feel like the cards were stacked against us from the beginning, and when we tried to get out of the vicious circle, it never worked.

At this point you have made progress, and know that your fear and anxiety from the past does not have to be carried into the present.

Scientifically, we know that the human brain can change. We can un-learn old irrational beliefs, and we can learn to believe what's rational and true about ourselves and our lives.

The world is really not a negative or a positive place. It all depends on your point of view.

You make "the world" into anything you want it to be by how you perceive it, and what you believe about it. What you believe about yourself and the world -- comes true.

Realistically, the world is a place where you fit and belong. We are all human beings and there is a place in this world where you are welcome. These are more rational thoughts than the "hostile world" thoughts we've believed in the past.

It's easy for a person with social anxiety to think that this is a negative world, after all the negative experiences we've had in life, and all the fearful emotions we've gone through.

But now, as a result of the journey we are on, we need to begin seeing the world and our life in a more realistic light.

Let's go conditional or neutral with our thinking.

Maybe I have more control over my emotions than I once thought.

Maybe I can un-learn some of my old irrational belief patterns and habits.

It's likely that as I continue on with therapy, my brain will continue to gradually change and shift in a realistic direction.

Maybe what I continually think to myself becomes true because I reinforce and re-play it so much.

Maybe the very same processes that kept my social anxiety alive are now going to be used to learn and believe rational things.

Maybe the world isn't such a bad place after all.

Maybe I have been reinforcing all the negativity I've lived through.

From now on, maybe I can do something different and reinforce the new rational attributes I am learning about myself.

Maybe I am not as bad off as I thought. Maybe my old brain habits led me to believe I was, and then trapped me into that negative cycle of thinking.

Maybe by relaxing, taking my time, and loosening up, I can feel calmer than I used to.

Maybe there's some truth to the idea that what I pay attention to – grows.

Maybe if I pay attention to the rational things I see and the rational explanations about my behavior, I will see the world in a different light, too.

Maybe this will happen. I'm not sure yet, but I see light at the end of the tunnel. It feels like something good is happening to me.

To move away from the "hostile world" view, start paying attention to the positive emotions you feel, and one of the best ways to do this is through any kind of relaxation or imaging method.

For example,

I close my eyes, take a deep breath, and slowly say:

"I am calm, relaxed, and feeling peaceful."

A more visual exercise would be more like this:

"I see the natural beauty all around me. The trees are green, the sky is blue, and there are multi-colored flowers lining my path. I am peacefully and calmly floating down a flowing, vibrant stream. Everything is calm and relaxed around me. I see everything in a beautiful, positive light and I continue to flow along the stream in perfect congruence with the world around me."

"I relax, loosen up my muscles, and lean into this calmness and peace.
I feel very much at home with my calmness and peace. I feel like I belong here. This place is my place and it is a place where I fit in."

You need to re-interpret, or at least consider, that social situations may potentially be good and positive for you. Let's approach it from the "glass is half full" perspective.

If we always feel **"separate from"** other people and the world around us, we never get over our feeling that the world is against us.

Luckily, your old thoughts and beliefs that led to feelings of social anxiety are growing weaker each and every time you "therapize." You can calmly look at social situations now and realize there is no instant panic in them. In fact, in most social engagements, there is potential for peace, harmony, and acceptance.

To stop viewing the world as a hostile place, practice your calming and slowing down techniques, and place a peaceful image in your mind. Talk to yourself calmly, and tell your brain what you want it to do. After a while, your perception of the world will change and become more realistic.

Deliberately make it a point to remember the good events, and the positive things that have happened in your life.

Even if you don't remember any, search a little more and expand your observations, and you can usually find events that were positive for you and where people treated you with friendship and respect.

Instead of focusing on the hostility of the world, it is healthier to focus on proactive, helpful thoughts and beliefs.

Think about these things and allow your calmness and peace to slowly change the way you view the world and the events in it.

Take it one step further and see your present and future life as becoming better. See yourself as happier as a result of your rational thoughts and beliefs.

Notice that you are enjoying life, interacting with other people that you like, and feeling satisfied.

The Good, the Better, and the Beautiful
What we decide to focus on becomes our world

Instead of only paying attention to negative and depressive things, we should pay more attention to the nice and the good things around us.

The title of this handout is a take-off of an old movie and song, but we've made the title more positive to indicate that we need to pay attention to the healthy and positive things happening all around us.

These are just suggestions, and you will have more of your own that you can add to this list. When you're fully engaged and paying attention to these positive things, we'll be putting another dent in the vicious circle of social anxiety.

Here are Some Suggestions:

1. **Sit down every day for a few minutes, allow yourself to relax with the method you prefer best, and imagine a beautiful place you have been.** Notice all the colorful details you can see. Add the details in if this makes it stronger for you. Notice how beautiful, peaceful, and serene this place really is.

    Any slowing down activity like this is helpful for us to do every day. We need to stay still and quiet and dwell on the good, the better, and the beautiful. We need to fill our mind with healthy, realistic, and positive thoughts. It's time we told ourselves the truth instead of noticing only negative things. There are always good, positive things happening, too.

2. **Go sit outside on the patio, in the backyard, at a park, or someplace else that is solitary and peaceful.** Focus on the beautiful things you see around you: flowers, trees, desert scenery, snow, the ocean, hills, mountains, lakes, fields, clouds, sky. Notice that being in nature can look invigorating, inviting, and beautiful, calm us down, and help us feel more relaxed and peaceful.

3. **Take a walk around the block or hike up a hill or mountain.** This is great physical exercise, but make sure you slow down to enjoy the beauty that you see all around you. Specifically, externally focus on all the beautiful, pretty, natural objects that cross your path.

4. **While you drive around town, drive in "slow driving" mode.** Use slow talk to speak to yourself so that your driving is not tension-filled and stressful. Deliberately notice and focus on the nice and beautiful things you see: beautiful yards, landscaping, an outstanding flower bed, a unique business establishment, beautiful architecture, and all the natural physical beauty that surrounds you.

In each and every case, the central message is to "stop and smell the roses." This is a lesson all of us need to learn – for our own enjoyment, peace, and tranquility.

The more we learn to FOCUS ON the good, the better, and the beautiful, the more our minds turn toward realistic perceptions of the world.

We all know there are good and bad things in the world, and there are many shades of gray in between.

Therefore, we have a decision to make:

   A. We can surrender to our "old" conditioning and continue to view the world as hostile and threatening to us, or

   B. We can gradually open up to the world and deliberately focus on the nice, peaceful, gentle, beautiful things that exist all around us.

This is one more strategy to help change our thinking about ourselves and the world. As we begin to see the world as a more benign place, we begin to see ourselves in a more peaceful and positive light.

You deserve to enjoy life and be happy.

You deserve to see yourself more realistically and rationally.

There is beauty in almost everything and the more you focus on the good, the better, and the beautiful, the more your perceptions of the world and of yourself will change.

Anxiety is a paradox, so:
Act Against Your Negative Feelings

This is one of the more difficult concepts to apply, but the thing to do is get started.

Once you start, and take the first step, every additional step becomes easier, and your rational emotions and positive feelings follow. You'll feel better faster.

Why should we let our emotions lie to us and keep us down in the dumps? If we're down and depressed, we can feel better immediately by acting against our negative emotions. Act against depression and anxiety by taking one step against it – by doing something active.

We're aware when our thoughts are irrational, but we tend to forget that our feelings can be irrational, too. Let me remind you to act, one step at a time, against your negative emotions.

Activity – taking action – is the solution to depression, but when we are depressed we don't feel like being active.

When hopelessness and helplessness control our lives, the only thing that can change things is exerting a little control by acting on the situation. If I nudge myself to take one step against my anxiety and depression, I feel better immediately. One active step makes me feel better, and makes it easier to take the next step.

Acting against our negative feelings means we do something we don't *feel* like doing at the time, because we *know* that if we take action, we will feel better afterwards.

This is counterintuitive and paradoxical, but explains why anxiety and depression are difficult to overcome.

The solution – the thing that will make you feel better – is in doing what you feel *least* like doing.

People who are depressed do not feel like getting up and becoming active. They feel hopeless, emotionless, and despondent. They want to lay in bed and dwell on their problems.

The solution to depression is action. By being active and busy, depression goes away. The solution to the depression is activity. The last thing a depressed person feels like doing is being active.

So the solution to the problem is both counterintuitive and paradoxical.

It is the same with anxiety. Your feelings and thoughts improve with action.

For social anxiety, we need to gently, in a step-by-step manner, work our way forward. We don't choose activities that cause too much anxiety to start with. If it frightens us to death, it is not a reasonable or rational starting-off point.

Instead, we choose something that causes just a little bit of anxiety, and we do it because we know it will help us feel better.

We choose to act against our negative emotions by doing something so that we can feel better.

We must nudge ourselves forward, with the belief secure in our brain that what we do not want to do – is the thing that will make us feel better. We know that once we get out of bed and act on the world, by doing something, we will feel better.

It is knowing we will feel better afterwards that makes this step possible.

If we act against our negative emotions, we eat away at our social anxiety. By doing this, it ensures our progress will be faster and more effective.

Acting against your negative emotions means "nudging" yourself to do something – when you don't feel like doing it. You know it's the right thing to do. Taking one step forward puts you in a better mood and saves you pain, misery, and despondency.

Once you fully understand this, the momentary pain of moving forward is easily forgotten as your depression evaporates and your mood goes up. You feel better again!

Why sit around and beat yourself up when we can do something about it instead? Why allow ourselves to be down and depressed when we can avoid days and hours of pain? Why allow depression and inaction to tear us down when we can feel better by taking one step forward?

Do not be passive. Move forward, one step at a time.

Anxious feelings and bad moods can be overcome, simply by taking action against them, and it takes only one step at a time.

We no longer must passively accept our negative moods and feelings. We can do something about them.

We can act against our negative feelings, one step at a time, and feel better as a result of it.

THE POWER STATEMENTS
(Rational Questions to Ask Yourself Every Day)

The following questions are good to ask yourself every day. You already know the answers to them, but it takes consistent reinforcement for the brain to fully take them in.

By asking rhetorical questions, we break up our old patterns of thinking and allow ourselves to consider new ideas and explanations. This is how our brain can believe what is rational about ourselves.

Questions:

1. Why should I let other people get under my skin?

2. Why should I let other people's thoughts bother me so much?

3. Why should everyone else's approval matter so much to me?

4. Do I need everyone's approval to feel OK about myself?

5. Why should I be dependent on the way other people see me?

The Power is Yours!

6. Will I crumble, fall, and die if someone doesn't like me?

7. Why do I give other people emotional power over me?

8. Why should I sweat, stew, and drive myself crazy over what other people think or say about me?

9. Is it possible that some people are negative about everything and don't like anyone?

10. Is it possible I don't need to make friends with everyone I meet?

11. Could it be that I don't need to expect everyone to like me?

We can be at home alone with our thoughts, and the ANTs come by for a visit. There is no one else in the room. The thoughts we have are our own thoughts. **Are they rational? Do they make any sense?**

They may have begun by other persons or other circumstances, but now it's *me* thinking these thoughts. I am generating my thoughts and the resulting emotions.

I need to decide whether I want to keep these irrational thoughts or not.

What is rational and what is not? I am the only one who has any control over what I choose to believe.

WHY SHOULD MY OWN THOUGHTS HURT ME?

WHY SHOULD I allow MY OWN THOUGHTS to HURT ME?

WHY SHOULD I ALLOW MY OWN THOUGHTS TO CAUSE ME EMOTIONAL PAIN?

Why should I beat myself up and dwell in my old ANTs garbage pile?

WHY SHOULD I ALLOW MY OWN THINKING TO bother me?

WHY DO I give OTHER PEOPLE POWER OVER ME?

The answers to these questions are obvious, and answering them has the power to keep the brain open to what is rational. These statements that you go over every day have the power to keep your brain thinking in a rational direction.

Make these statements to yourself each day and review them when you read this handout:

> "I AM FINE AND O.K. with myself – I don't need other people's approval for me to like and accept myself."

> "I need to ask myself these questions every day, so that the answer will pop automatically into my mind when my thoughts go negative on me."

It's good to remind ourselves of what the brain needs to hear. This statement is true.

You are OK in life's situations. You are not perfect and you have problems, like everyone else. You've learned to accept yourself for who you are, and realize you are as good as everyone else.

There is nothing wrong with you, with the exception that you have been viewing yourself incorrectly for most of your life.

> ANTS never tell the truth. Their mission is to trap and trick me.

Why should I let ANTs run and ruin my life?

Ask yourself these questions every day. Your brain will recognize that these are all irrational thoughts. Even though you already know they're irrational, by asking these questions, you break up the irrational fire-and-wire connections in the brain, and you reinforce rational thinking.

Behavioral Experiments:
Staying in the Moment

When you are doing behavioral experiments in public, take a group member or a social anxiety friend along with you, if possible.

Anyone who understands what you are doing and why you're doing it can be a good support system for you. But even without an understanding friend, you can do these experiments on your own, provided you start out reasonably, and rationally process what you're doing.

If you don't have a friend with you, make sure you plan the experiment out well and commit it to paper so that you can follow up on it later on. This helps you stay organized and keeps you rational before, during, and after the experiment.

Find an experiment that causes only a little nervousness – one in which you know you can be rational about after you're done.

Here's an example:

- I'm going to the shopping mall today to use the look-around technique, so that I can see what's really going on around me. I'll see if using the look around technique (LAT) reduces my self-consciousness when other people are around me in the mall.

If you gently look around as you're walking through the mall, the experiment should only cause you a little bit of anxiety (one step forward), so the next thing to realize is that we should be externally focused and stay in the moment as long as we need to – until we feel our anxiety begin to subside.

It is the normal tendency to do an experiment quickly and get it over with as soon as possible. That may be OK when we first start our behavioral experiments, but now, as you get into a pattern of practicing them, you can waste a lot of time when you end the experiment too quickly, for the sake of getting it over.

You have committed yourself to doing the experiment, so let's take our time with it so that it really sinks in as to what is happening around us.

By doing an experiment and staying with it longer, we give ourselves the opportunity to *feel* anxiety going down. Giving ourselves the time to allow this to happen speeds up our rate of recovery.

Ask yourself these questions:

Are people really as judgmental and critical as I've thought? What kinds of expressions do they have on their faces? Are they openly hostile or subtly negative? What is really going on? Is it possible that what I expect to happen – is not happening at all? Is it possible I didn't need to feel self-conscious? How many people are staring at me? How many people are noticing me for longer than two seconds?

Stay in the moment and carry out the experiment for a longer amount of time. Try not to just do it for 10 seconds and then escape. See if you can stay in the moment longer, so that your anxiety has a chance to drop.

For example, if you're in the mall and you're projecting your voice from one floor to another (you need a friend for this), look around to see what other people who heard you are doing, and then *stay where you are* for a longer period of time so that you can see what people are doing after you called out to your friend on the second story.

If you are by yourself, do something that will single you out for attention, like drop your change, or have problems with the credit card swipe. Look around gently and see how angry people are with you or if they are paying attention to you or not.

Stay with this experiment for a longer period of time so that everything readjusts nicely, and you can feel your anxiety go down, before moving out of the situation.

Staying in the moment means to stay where you are and keep using the look around technique longer. By staying in the moment you have a longer amount of time to really see what dropping your change did.

When you did it, it may have made you feel more self-conscious, but did other people gaze at you intently? How many? If they did notice, how many of them are still looking at you? How many are looking at you with judgment on their faces? How many negative comments did you get? Did the mall security come and escort you out of the mall?

Stay in the moment so that you can get the full effect of what really happened.

See if you can wait, using the look-around technique, until you feel your anxiety go down. Stay in the moment, be the potential center of attention for a few seconds, and continue using the look around technique.

As you begin to see what's really going on around you, your anxiety will go down. See if you can stay with your experiment until you feel this change occurring.

You slow down the experiment to give your brain the additional time to process what's going on. In this situation, look around, take your time, and see what is actually happening.

Additional suggestions for experiments:

- Ask a salesperson for help and make small talk with them as you find what you're looking for.

- Ask for directions on how to find a store, and stay with the conversation until you get a detailed explanation of how to get there that you can follow. Ask more questions if needed.

- Talking with people you feel comfortable with, go into an area you've never discussed before, maybe something topical that has to do with humanitarian interests, like educating children or helping the poor. Stay with the conversation longer so that any apprehension you had has a chance to go down.

- When you wave a greeting from your car, do it with strangers to see how they'll respond. Some will ignore you, and some will respond in kind, but the point is to stay with the experiment longer and get the full effect on anxiety concerning what you're doing.

Any circumstance you turn into an experiment in your own life can be done in this way. Stick with the situation for a longer amount of time, until you can feel the anxiety drop.

Do these experiments, like we talked about, every day.

Self-Statements:
Moving in a Positive Direction

I am a proficient and capable person in my own areas of knowledge.

I am learning to accept and believe in myself – just the way I am.

I don't have to "change" to be a good person.

I am a unique and special person in the sense that there is no one else just like me anywhere in the world. Who knows what I might be able to contribute as I get older?

I have special talents that are above average – I am particularly good at some things – and I can teach them to other people when they need help.

I am learning to accept the different parts of my personality, and to change the parts I want to change.

I don't have to prove myself to anyone. I don't have to prove myself to myself.

My feelings and my needs are important too. I am just as important as anyone else.

It's O.K. to think about what I'd like and need. It's not being selfish to seek peace and calmness for myself.

It's necessary for me to make some time for myself each day.

I believe in my capabilities, and value the talents I can offer the world.

I am sincere.

I believe I can make progress toward my goals.

I am a valuable and important person, worthy of the respect of others.

Others see me in a better light than I thought.

When the people I chose to be friends with get to know me, they like me.

There are people who enjoy being around me right now. They like to hear what I have to say and know what I think. Even if this hasn't happened yet, I am moving in this general direction.

Perhaps others recognize that I have a lot to offer, even when I don't recognize this myself.

I am slowly and steadily overcoming social anxiety.

I can always be proactive. I can look at my options and make the most rational decision.

I deserve to be loved by the people I love.

I'm learning to accept assistance and help from other people.

I'm optimistic about my life now. I look forward to new challenges and enjoy them.

I know what my values are and I am confident about the decisions I make.

It's easier to accept legitimate compliments and praise from other people.

I take pride in what I've accomplished, and look forward to what I am going to achieve.

Avoidance:
Our Worst Enemy

The biggest obstacle to our progress is something we've been doing most of our lives: avoiding things because they cause us anxiety.

It is natural that when we're anxious, we avoid. It is also natural that when we have avoided situations for many years, this avoidance becomes a habit.

For example, we may be avoiding some events today more out of habit than because of anxiety. Nevertheless, it is avoidance of situations that keeps us stuck in our old habits. We can never move forward in life if we continue to avoid.

It is also easier to avoid if other people enable us to avoid. For example, it is becoming increasingly more common for parents to allow their children to avoid having friends and doing things outside the house.

The more avoidant a young person becomes, the more they fear the things they have not done. So, they may choose avoidance rather than progress because it is the easiest thing to do – it is the path of least resistance.

The bottom line here is that no one overcomes social anxiety who consistently avoids.

To get better, we need to be gently proactive. This is a step-by-step incremental process – no flooding – but nevertheless we are making progress. We no longer choose to avoid everything, just because it causes anxiety.

Gently and persistently, we are choosing to meet our social challenges, one at a time, while thinking as rationally as possible about them.

(Here again, we must put the cognitive therapy beliefs together with the behavioral therapy we are doing.)

So, **be proactive. Prove to yourself that your fears are usually groundless**.

Start any new activity slowly. For example, say hello to new and different people, initiate small talk conversations when you feel ready, telephone a group member and arrange to do something together, do experiments at the shopping mall with the group or a friend.

Being less avoidant and more proactive is another big paradox. Therefore, we need to learn many different ways to avoid avoidance. This is the main purpose of behavioral therapy.

"I am going to take the strategies I learn in cognitive therapy and gently begin to DO them in my daily life. I am tired of avoiding and being stuck in my anxiety. I choose to avoid avoidance in a rational way."

Avoiding avoidance – in a step by step, gentle way – is a central theme in overcoming social anxiety.

It is a theme we cannot avoid if we want to get better.

Irrational Expectations Are Killers:
Stay Away at All Costs

We do not want to "set ourselves up" ahead of time for failure and defeat. It isn't logical to expect things to happen in irrational ways.

We can't try, "force" or "pressure" anything to happen on a rigid time schedule. Instead, we should move ahead gently and peaceably.

Maybe I'm expecting a raise at work because I've worked there the mandatory time for advancement at my job.

So I say to myself:

> ➢ *"Today, I will go to work, march into the bosses' office, and get that raise I deserve so much."*

Maybe this is how it should work, and maybe you deserve the raise, but there are too many variables beyond your control in this situation. By having the irrational expectation that you should get a raise now, you are not only being irrational, but you're being inflexible.

You are seeing things from your point of view, and you're not considering other perspectives of the situation.

In this situation, the potential is there for you to set yourself up for a fall, and it is likely that you will have one.

Maybe your company is no longer giving anyone raises. They consider you a good employee, and they don't want to lose you. But what if company policies establish that no raises are given for the next six months due to economic hardship?

If you take this personally and allow yourself to feel defeated because you didn't get the raise, you are sabotaging your own life and your own feelings.

Your expectations of what should happen are not something written in stone that *will* happen. It pays to keep our expectations rational.

Being turned down for a raise is not a slap in the face in this situation. This would occur to anyone asking for a raise during this time. You are taking things too personally and expecting too much out of a situation in which you have little control.

Or, consider this irrational expectation: "Tonight I will go out and meet someone and start a romantic relationship."

This is a big, bold, unrealistic expectation. Why?

You can go out and "meet" someone tonight, but the underlying expectation is that you'll meet someone you're sexually attracted to and develop a relationship with. Because you desire this so much, you want this to happen tonight. You have set yourself up for failure by expecting irrational outcomes.

The trouble is that you do not have control over WHO is going to be "out there" and when they're going to be out there. The specific type of person you're interested in likely makes the task more difficult.

This particular expectation is usually a real killer: you expect too much to happen, too quickly, and the situation is out of your control.

You set yourself up for defeat if you expect life to work this way.

Instead, a healthier, more productive outlook is to generally increase your social activities in areas in which you are already interested. If you like singing, join a chorus. If you want to talk about books, join a book club.

If you're into computing and specific aspects of computers or the internet, there are groups of people that are interested in that. There are meet up groups on the internet for almost any interest you can imagine.

Your interest in the activity should come *first*, and your focus should be on having a good time. It should not be on the people who might be there, or on finding the right person for a relationship.

If your focus is on slowly expanding your social activities, you have increased your chances of reaching your goal, because you haven't set up any rigid, irrational expectations.

This is another paradox. The more desperately you seek something and try to force it to happen, the more elusive it becomes.

If your expectations about life are irrational, and you see things from only your own point of view, what you expect is not going to happen. Our expectations must be in line with reality.

If I go out tonight, my focus should be on *enjoying events* with friends, from having dinner, to taking in a movie, to swimming on the beach, or to clubbing. You can be open to meeting a person you're sexually attracted to and that's fine, but to expect that it will happen on your rigid time schedule is irrational.

Instead, **focus on moving forward for your own benefit,** and expand your social network gradually.

Take away any pressure you feel relating to time, so that you can develop rational and logical expectations and plans.

Open up your mind so that you can see the situation from all different angles and perspectives. Think this through logically, ahead of time, and be rational with yourself. Be patient so that you can correct your misperceptions and allow your expectations to be logical and rational.

DON'T LET YOUR (IRRATIONAL) EXPECTATIONS GET THE BETTER OF YOU.

HAVE A RATIONAL TALK WITH YOURSELF EVERY DAY

You have already started this strategy by reading the handouts over to yourself calmly, which allows you to understand the strategies better and prepares you to begin using them in your life.

Sit down, when you are alone, and talk out loud to yourself calmly.
Use slow talk to calm yourself down and keep negative emotions away, so that the rational talk you have with yourself stays in the forefront of the conversation.

Talking out loud to yourself like this, during your 30 minute study time, is powerful. You are restating what you have done, your brain hears and makes sense of it, and all that's left to do is to congratulate yourself for doing a good job.

We are not going to be influenced by negative emotions, like anxiety, when we have a rational talk with ourselves. We stay *rational* – because we're paying attention to the truth.

Remind yourself of all the things you're doing to get better. This is rational talk, and what you're speaking out loud is a fact. For example:

- I used the look around technique at work this week to prove to myself that no one was judging or scrutinizing me.

- I took the initiative and started a conversation with a new person today. We made some simple small talk, but I remembered to slow down, take the pressure off myself, and relax.

- I did OK with the presentation I had to make yesterday. I remembered to approach the situation with the expectation that I would do OK, relaxed my muscles, and talked calmly through each of my points. I didn't rush anything.

> I stayed in the moment and allowed myself to experience anxiety going down.

As I've said before, most of the time other people aren't around to tell us when we've done a good job, so we need to do it ourselves – in a way that the brain will remember.

When you use the strategies, and do what you need to do, it's important to talk this out and congratulate yourself afterwards. You are stating rational facts, and your brain hears and believes what you say to it.

Inside the brain, the neurons are rearranging themselves based on what you just did. In the past, presentations meant anxiety. Now, presentations mean calmness, slowing down, and staying in the moment. The neurons in the brain change a little each time you apply the strategies to activities in your own life.

Because feelings are so powerful and strong, we must remember to talk to ourselves rationally every day.

Find a place and a time, usually during your 30 minute study time, and slow yourself down. Talk to yourself rationally about what is happening in your life.

For example, you could say:

- *"Today, I felt some anxiety when I introduced myself to the new workers at my job. So I will slow it down next time, and remind myself to use slow talk when I talk with other people. I know that as I calm myself down in public, my anxiety will continue to go down."*

By staying in slow talk mode, and calming yourself down, you will be able to keep your thinking rational too.

Talking to yourself rationally – making this a daily practice – adds strength and weight to overcoming social anxiety.

POISONOUS THOUGHTS

Anxious, worrying thoughts which lead to anxious, worrying feelings create the traumatic, anxiety-ridden lives of those of us who suffer from social anxiety.

It is when we become aware of this, and begin to take control of our thoughts, which lead to feelings, that we can overcome this downward spiral of negativity.

This "expecting the worst to happen" syndrome – that keeps our anxieties alive – must be stopped.

This is how we've responded to anxiety in the past:

We rehearsed our failures repeatedly.

We told ourselves we can't do things.

We told ourselves that the things we can do are horrible, awful, and we hate them.

We told ourselves we'll never get any better... We say, "I've always been like this..."

We keep reinforcing the negative, the scary – the obsessive thoughts... the fearful feelings... and then we continue to have anxiety, worry, and fear.

Do you see what's going on?

Thoughts have no power to change things in and of themselves... You give them power because of what you believe.

Thoughts require action on your part. For example, try running your computer with just your thoughts, or go to the grocery store and shop with only your thoughts, or write an e-mail using only your cognitive abilities.

Thinking, by itself, is not enough.
Every thought requires action to give it life.

If our thought is irrational, the powerless thought creates great damage to our lives when we act on it.

If you act on an irrational thought, you turn things that aren't really true into the truth. You created it by thinking, but then you acted on it and believed it. You have made this powerless thought come true.

Here are some examples:

Thought: "I am afraid to speak in front of other people."
Action: Worry about it. Avoid. Have anticipatory anxiety.
Belief: My fear grows stronger. My negative beliefs are stronger. It seems impossible that I can ever speak in front of other people.

If you *dismiss* the thought before you act on it, you'll be OK. Thoughts have no power in and of themselves.

But if you *reinforce* the irrational thought, take it in, and repeat it to yourself and others, you've added *action* to the thought and, as a result, you believe it. You took an irrational thought and made it come true because you paid attention and acted on it.

Let's look at another example:

Thought: I am not as good as other people.
Action: I continually say "I can't do this" and "I can't do that" to myself and other people.
Belief: I am set in my belief that I have cannot do most things. I've been saying this for years: Other people are better than me.

Again, if you dismiss the thought as being irrational and go on to something else, you'll be OK. But, if you *act* on the irrational thought, you make it come true. When you rehearse an irrational thought and replay it over and over again, it makes it easier for you to act on it. The irrational belief becomes true.

We make our thoughts come true when we act on them.

How do we stop the chain of poisonous thinking?

1. I need to stop irrational thoughts immediately, and move on to something healthier and proactive.

2. I don't want to give irrational thoughts room to grow. If I suspect my thinking is irrational, I label it as a lie and dismiss it at the same time.

3. If it is a persistent thought or a long-held belief, I turn the tables on the ANTs and think about it in a different way. I open my mind to alternative explanations and logical reasoning.

4. An awareness of what one irrational thought can do to my life steers me toward dismissing it immediately.

"I will dismiss an irrational thought immediately. I know that if I don't act on irrational thinking, I give the irrational thought no room to grow."

Add the "take the easiest road" approach and turning the tables on the ANTs to deal with poisonous thoughts.

> "Dealing with other people may be anxiety causing now,
> but when I talk to people using the 'take the easiest step' approach,
> I'll do OK. It's certainly not the end of the world."

Proactive Act: Carry the rational thoughts through and speak to one or two other people. Go slowly, but keep on going.

You must gently question your ANTs beliefs, thinking patterns, and thinking strategies.

"Are they telling me the rational truth and leading me in a healthy, helpful direction? Or, do they keep me in a cycle of defeat, depression, avoidance, fear, and "expecting the worst to happen?"

Keep your brain open to all possibilities, and your brain will reorganize itself for you in a logical, rational way and you will get the answer that you want.

Worry...
Leads to More Worry and More Worry and More Worry and...

Worry is never positive. It never does any good. There is no redeeming value in worry.

Worrying is an ANT-like process. It always leads me in the wrong direction. It always exaggerates.

It always blows things out of proportion and consumes my every thought. Worry leaves a trail of anxiety and depression behind it.

Worry only leads me to worry more. Worry fuels the fire of anxiety and causes more worry.

Nothing good ever comes from worrying. Most of what I worry about never happens anyway. Worry just makes things worse.

It throws me and my progress off track. Worry is another lying ANT. It is incapable of telling me the truth.

Worry wants me to be irrational, to expect the very worst, and to see the situation as being catastrophic. Worry is always negative. If I surrender to worry, I leave myself with no solution.

Worry needs to be stopped – dead cold – in its tracks. It is a lie. It has no basis in fact.

Worry never solves problems. It only creates them. The more I worry, the more problems I have.

Worry is a negative emotion, and can only fuel other negative emotions. There is no help, no progress, and no solution in worrying.

Worry robs me of my minute, my hour, and my day. Worry keeps me living in the troubling past or the fearful future. Worry makes sure that the time I spend with it is miserable and depressing.

Worry sets me up for defeat, anxiety, stress, fear, and sickness. It never does me any good. It always wants to trip me up and knock me down.

Worry needs to be stopped. I need to stop worry. It will throw any dark filter over reality that it can find – and it is always bad and unhealthy for me.

What can I do about it? If I'm worried about something, and can do something about it, I'll do it. I'll stop the thinking and start the doing. Problem solved.

But, if I have no control over the situation and what I'm worrying about, my worry will do no good anyway. It will only depress me and pull me down into the vicious maze of social anxiety.

Worrying never solves a thing. There is no solution in worry. There is only misery and defeat. Excessive thinking (worrying) is like poison. Catch it, stop it, and move away from it.

Say to yourself: "Worry never does me any good. It is only there to hurt me and rob me of my peace. Therefore, I deliberately choose to do something else…"

Then, go and do something. Find something fun and interesting and do it. Or, as you progress, rely upon the rational statements that you are making a part of your daily life.

"So what? Who cares? WHY am I dwelling on this?" "It's no big deal."

Worry is a fraud and a liar. Nothing good ever comes from worry.

It's time for us to put worry in its place. Stop the thinking by using any cognitive method or strategy that works, and then move on.

Feelings, Feelings, and More Feelings

Question: Why do I have anxiety about so many different things?

Answer: You have anxiety so that you can learn to stop thinking about it.

Q: That isn't an answer. What do you mean?

A: The anxious feelings are there so that you can stop asking, "Why are these anxious feelings here?" "Why do I have them?" "Will I always be like this?" "Won't they ever go away?" "Will I ever have a life?" Don't ask those questions because they just cause you to have more anxiety.

Q: I don't understand. What do you mean?

A: The more you ask questions like, "Why are these anxious feelings here?" the more they will be here.

Q: And the less I notice them and ask about these feelings, the less they will be there?

A: That's right. It's another paradox. We need to do the opposite of what our old neural pathway systems tell us to do. Overcoming social anxiety involves counterintuitive, paradoxical strategies.

Q: But isn't thinking about positive things good to do?

A: Yes, if you're thinking about positive events or situations or planning for something proactive and forward-moving. But if it's thinking that dwells on the past or on your problems, this kind of thinking is a red flag because it always pulls you down. If you start to feel anxious, stop the thinking and start the doing. Get your mind off the ANTs lies.

Q: Won't thinking help me come to a conclusion? Can't I figure out why I have ANTs?

A: **No.** Thinking about anxiety will only make you more anxious. You will come to the conclusion that there is no conclusion. You will still be stuck asking these questions forever.

There are no rational answers to questions that come from over-thinking and over-analyzing. Millions of people worldwide are still trying to figure out why they have such crippling anxiety. They've been trying to figure this out all their lives.

Most never come to an adequate conclusion, and the ones who do, are *not* better off than when they started. Actively working on getting better is the only road that helps us get better.

Q: So, what should I do?

A: First, stop, slow down, take a deep breath, and realize that all you have to do is accept your positive emotions, such as calmness and peace.

Q: What do you mean "Accept?"

A: **Accept it.** You don't have to do anything. Lean back into your chair and accept yourself and your positive emotions, such as calmness and peace. As you accept it, you have stopped fighting, battling, struggling, trying, pushing, forcing, or attacking. Because you choose to accept, everything becomes easier -- and you make faster progress against anxiety.

Q: OK, don't fight. Then, I need to accept? What should I do next?

A: **Let the anxiety go, release it, walk through it, and move on with your life.** Don't sit around and ruminate on your problems. Get on with your daily activities and your daily life.

Q: The more I accept myself, the more the anxiety goes away?

A: **Exactly. Calm, peaceful, acceptance has great power.** The more you accept yourself and move forward with your life, the more time you have to focus on good, constructive things to do. If you don't pay attention to it, it doesn't have any power over you and it can't stay alive.

We are being reminded of the anxiety paradox again.

- The more I can accept, move on, act, find distractions, and turn the tables on the ANTs, the less anxiety will be able to bother me. The more the strategies and statements become automatic thoughts and behaviors, the less anxiety can interfere with our progress. I am in the process of calmly and peacefully defeating social anxiety permanently.

- Instead of letting my emotions run away with me, and get me to start acting and believing irrational things, I need to make sure I have a realistic grip on my life. I am in control of my emotions and my life. Continuing to wallow in the mud with my negative emotions is only making things worse.

- Negative emotions are damaging to my progress and my proactivity. Negative emotions lead me to think irrationally and illogically, and I do and say things that aren't even true.

- Negative emotions need to be **stopped**, as quickly as possible, so that we can think rationally, logically, and clearly.

Shyness, Timidity, and Being Hesitant

We need to work on reducing our shyness and timidity, and learn to feel OK about speaking up, talking about our interests, and just being a part of the group.

I was in graduate school later in life than most people, so I was around 38 years old when this happened. I had been given the assignment of being a teaching assistant for the undergraduate educational psychology program. I was teaching one of the popular modules – "Motivational Psychology."

On the first day of class we had to take our 500 students and split them up into smaller groups based on which modules they wanted to take. I had never been in charge of an orientation like this before, so I followed the graduate student program director to one of the rooms.

She and I walked together to the classroom where we would be running the orientation session. As we walked through the door of the crowded classroom, **what she did next was something that burned into my brain immediately.**

She walked through the door, noticed the classroom was entirely full, and then just raised her voice a little so that everyone could hear her, and nonchalantly talked to them – as she was making her way to the front of the room. She sounded pleasant, and no one was in any doubt about who was in charge of that room.

All she said was, **"Good morning, everyone. Are you all here for our junior-level psychology class?"** She was positive and upbeat, and the student responses were positive and upbeat. I sat down in the chair in the front of the room and just watched and listened to her. She had just done something I thought I could never do... and she had done it easily.

Her voice was smooth, calming, and professional, and elicited a positive response from the students. I was expecting some complaining about the courses available and some negativity, but there was none.

I see now that my brain was skewed negatively and I just expected something to go wrong. But when she walked into the room, **she took charge by being positive and upbeat, and the students responded to her in the same way.** Wow. What a surprise it was for me! Here's what I learned from this experience socially:

Extend yourself just a little more when you can, find small talk things to talk about that feel comfortable to you and keep using them. Lower the pitch of your voice slightly and develop a more "no big deal" or "who cares" attitude that can be heard when you speak.

People want you to be expressive and talkative, especially if you are in charge of anything. They are uncomfortable with hesitancy and quietness. People like it when you feel completely relaxed and comfortable because this allows them to feel comfortable, too.

Rationally, you have plenty to talk about, even though anxiety might have stifled you in the past. You are intelligent and know a lot about many things. Express your thoughts and emotions, say things, and get out of your head so that you can verbalize what's on your mind.

Hesitancy in your voice: See if you can end most of your sentences on a "down-note." In other words, your last sentence or phrase should be **declarative** in nature. You are making a relevant statement, so your voice goes down slightly.

If you were introducing yourself, you would say "I am John Smith and I come from London, England." Your voice would go down as you said "...London, England." You are making a statement that is true. There doesn't need to be any question or hesitancy in what you say. You have made a declarative statement, so your voice goes down.

If your sentences don't end on a "down note," you sound too tentative, too wishy-washy to the other person, like you're not sure what you're saying. You sound too *indecisive*. See if you can slow yourself down, relax, and use slow talk to add the "who cares?" attitude to your voice and the "down note" to the end of your sentence.

Not only will you sound better and clearer; you will sound more professional and authoritative. People will respect you more just because you talked to them in this manner.

Talk more, at length, to people. Make declarative statements. Stay away from raising your voice at the end of sentences so that everything sounds like a question.

Speak up whenever you want, speak up when you hadn't planned it, and take a proactive step (just one) against the ANTs.

People like it when you are more expressive and talk. Your words do not have to be entertaining. They do not have to be interesting to everyone. You have EVERY RIGHT to talk just like anyone else does, so please take advantage of this right.

Allow yourself to make mistakes, without beating yourself up.

Shyness, timidity, and being hesitant can change by using these strategies. Practice on them at home when you're by yourself if you need to feel more comfortable talking this way. I know that when I heard my friend in graduate school, open the classroom door and breeze to the front of the room, it was a situation I would never forget. In just five seconds, she had them all on track, all in a good mood, and all of them willing to cooperate.

She expected them to react in this logical way, and they did. It worked because she took control of the situation, walked in confidently, and started talking. She was in control. She did not hide behind the podium or use me as a crutch. I doubt if anyone knew I was even there. She just naturally breezed in and took over – after all, it was her job to be in charge.

Shyness, timidity, and being hesitant make things worse, and hold us back. If we gently meet the situation in front of us, and do what we need to do unapologetically, we'll make a great impact on the situation. Our expectations come true because we are not so hesitant and timid to accept our successes.

I can sum this up by saying, "It's not rational to hesitate and be so timid. It never helps us, and gives off an inaccurate portrayal of who we are. Instead, I gently move forward, accept my responsibilities in the situation, and am OK with it. No fake bashfulness, hesitancy, or inhibitions."

Instead, I step forward and meet life, expecting the best to happen. As I move forward, in a friendly manner, expecting the best to happen, I make it happen. My days of hesitancy and timidity are gone. Now I can live life.

Therapy Strategies That Seem Small...
But Have Really Powerful Results

Think about these suggestions and make a change when it helps:

- **Do some cognitive therapy in the morning**... before your day starts. Remind yourself of what's accurate. Talk it out loud to yourself. Your self-talk is becoming the way you think. Your day will go better if you start it out with rational thinking.

- **Your brain believes what it hears you say repeatedly, over and over again.** Your brain doesn't know the difference between something that is "irrational" and something that is "rational." The brain is neutral. So, tell your brain what is rational. Fill it up with what is true, helpful, and healthy.

- **Sing, hum, talk out loud to your radio, your mp3 player, or yourself.** Call a positive friend and talk to positive people in your environment.

- **Be friendly to people on the way to work or school.** Wave or acknowledge people even if it seems small. Take the initiative and do it first. Say "hi" at least, when you do not feel like carrying on a conversation.

- **Stick a pencil sideways in your mouth for fifteen minutes a day when you are alone** (Do not get the lead into your mouth). Doing this affects your facial muscles, and your muscles then affect your brain (i.e., the way you feel). A silly and often stupid-sounding exercise like this works because it affects the muscles in your face and your brain's neural pathway systems.

- **Be a little more physically active even if you are at work.** Take the stairs instead of the elevator. Move around calmly instead of just sitting in the same position, or running around like a chicken with its head cut off.

- **Exercise every day.** If you are physically healthy, get outside or go to the gym and do something that gets your heart beating quickly for 30 minutes a day. This is a major "help" to overcoming social anxiety – and one that gets left out of the therapy mixture way too often. Check with your doctor first if you have a health condition, but most people can exercise for twenty to thirty minutes a day. This burns off excess adrenaline and cortisol.

- **Activity, specifically proactivity, is needed.** These are small things, small steps, and only one at a time. But you must do something small at first, and you need to repeat it... Over and over again. "Nudge" yourself to act, even though you don't feel like it, because you know you'll feel better once you've acted. Nudging yourself forward, one step at a time, is the right way to go about it.

- **Overlearning is the only way to change the brain.** So, the repetition of small things will gradually become automatic new beliefs. Small steps today allow for bigger steps tomorrow.

- **Warm yourself up in the morning before you go to school or work.** Sing, hum, or wave to yourself in the mirror. "Fake" smile at yourself, and it won't feel fake anymore. Open yourself up. Get the tiredness out. Warming yourself up is especially important for people who live alone and don't have human contact until they get to school or work.

Seeing Things from a Different Perspective

Looking at things from other points of view can help us learn to accept the truth about ourselves. If I have a problem viewing myself accurately, I can look at it from another perspective. What would other people say? How do other people feel about it? What would other people think?

One of the deserving statements that typically takes longer to resolve is **"I deserve to like myself, to respect myself, and to accept myself for who I am."** Many people believe it is rational, but they don't feel that they deserve to accept themselves because of what's been done or said to them in the past.

Keri was one of those people who understood that it was rational to like and respect herself, but she didn't feel like she deserved it.

"Keri," I said to her quietly, "Do you think the other members of the group should be able to accept themselves and respect themselves for who they are?"

This took her by surprise. "Well, yes," she said, "of course. They're all nice people and all of them deserve to believe that about themselves."

I glanced at her again. "If you can say that and mean it, then would it surprise you to hear that the other group members would say the same thing about you?"

She struggled a little bit with that question, but quickly realized that if the other group members were asked, they would agree that she deserved to feel good and accept herself, too.

"If we went around the room, person by person," I continued, "and asked the other group members if you deserve to accept yourself or not, I expect we'd get a unanimous answer from them." Keri nodded quietly, taking this all in.

A solution to problems like this is to consider external sources, instead of relying on our own internal beliefs. Remember that it's our own internal beliefs that have kept social anxiety alive in the first place.

It's more likely that external sources are reliable in matters like this. We already know we are prone to internally skewed views about ourselves.

This way of looking at things could be called "If the Situation is Not About me..." **meaning it's very easy to see what is rational when you look at other people and take yourself out of the situation.**

It's easy to look at others and make a rational judgment. But when *you* are in the picture, things aren't quite so clear. Your old negative beliefs about yourself may still be harsh and judgmental.

It was easier for Keri to see that she deserved to respect and accept herself once she looked at it from another viewpoint. She understood that everyone else in the group deserved to accept and like themselves, and logically, she did, too. By looking at the situation from other people's viewpoints, it made things more personal and was easier to see what was rational.

You can ask yourself questions like this to come to a rational conclusions and beliefs about yourself:

- "Why don't you deserve to like yourself, to respect yourself, to accept yourself? Everyone else accepts themselves. Do you think they can accept you, too?"
- "Why, if you can accept them, are you so different?"
- "What would other people say about this?"
- "How would other people assess your actions?"

If everyone else you know deserves to be respected, then you do, too. The logic is just so strong, powerful, and overwhelming that the weight of this logic helps us to be rational with ourselves as well.

- I am just as good as anyone else. I am not better than, or worse than other people.

- Looking at situations from other people's points of view is always valuable. Subtracting yourself from the situation helps you see reality in a situation.

Turning it upside-down and looking at it from every angle helps, too. By asking questions like these, Keri learned to peacefully accept herself and feel that she deserved to feel OK about herself, too.

Fully accepting ourselves is another day-by-day process, but Keri accomplished this by getting as rational as she possibly could, and then mentally taking herself out of the situation.

She saw that every other group member deserved to accept themselves, no matter who they were or how much social anxiety they had. By putting herself back into the situation, she realized that if everyone else had the right to accept themselves, then she had that right, too.

If any other group member had been asked if Keri deserved to accept herself, the person would quickly say "yes, of course!" The strength of the argument is then indisputable, and she could quietly sit, say to herself that she *did* deserve to respect herself, and do it without the resistance inside that anxiety was trying to cause.

Looking at problems from different points of view helps us clarify what is true about ourselves. Keri began to look at acceptance in this way. All she did was think it through rationally and reinforce her thoughts daily. It was just a fact – a very clear one, and one that Keri came to believe and feel about herself. Feeling that she deserved to accept and like herself made a big difference in her mood and in her judgment of herself.

The fact of the matter is that if all human beings have the right to like, value, respect, and accept themselves, then Keri does, too. Once she thought this through, she could calmly accept this – and stop fighting against it.

When she fully accepted this rational idea, the feelings she had about herself changed. Keri wanted to feel good about herself – and she was prepared for change. She was prepared for believing and feeling the truth. She wasn't playing games.

If someone is not ready to believe and feel what is rational, they put up walls of resistance that we sometimes call defense mechanisms.

Sometimes this happens early in therapy and it takes longer for the resistance to go away and the rationality to kick in.

When you run into a situation like this – where you know something is rationally accurate, but you seem unable to be able to feel it emotionally, here's what to do:

Imagine all the positive people in your life that deserve to believe every one of the "Deserving Statements." Mentally go through this list of anyone who is a positive, supportive person and who deserves to feel that way. Then, turn the situation around on yourself, and ask "Do they feel that way about me? Do they think I deserve to believe the 'Deserving Statements?' Do they feel I should accept myself?"

By doing this, you see that each and every one of those people would answer with a quick "yes." There would be no hesitation on their part.

The hesitation is on your part. It is YOU who is having a hard time with accurate and rational feelings. Rely on your own rationality and common sense. Run through the list of people in your mind and, if you need to, directly ask them the question, "Do you think I deserve to _____? Why?"

It makes sense to do this with someone who is going through the same therapy and has social anxiety, but you understand the point I am making.

Going through this exercise adds a certain weight to your deliberations and really lets you see what you deserve to feel. Quietly and peacefully, sit back and accept the rational truth. As you accept the truth without mental reservations, you start to feel what you deserve to feel.

Don't force or pressure anything… just have that rational talk with yourself every day and sit back quietly – and peacefully take in what you have learned. As you do this, your emotions begin to change, and you will get the chance to FEEL what your rationality has already told you.

STAY OUT OF THE TWILIGHT ZONE
Move into the "Peace Zone"

We will use the term "peace zone" to indicate our ability to use our positive emotions to feel calmness, peace, and relaxation.

The peace zone handouts help us increase our positive emotions and put them in charge of our day. You can decide to enter the peace zone and stay away from the negative emotions you learned and became a habit over time.

Like the automatic negative thinking we're breaking up and interrupting, we are also interrupting the association between events and the *emotions* they cause. We can replace negative emotions with positive emotions by learning to feel calmness and peace.

Here are some suggestions that allow us feelings of calmness and peacefulness:

1. **When you are not feeling anxious, practice going into the "peace zone."** Do this when you're alone, at first, during your thirty minute study time. Even though you are not feeling anxious at that given time, you still choose to move into your "peace zone." By allowing yourself to feel more calmness and relaxation, you are creating a new habit as you relax and calm down, and continue to do it.

You do not have to read a handout to do this.
You do not have to be listening to an audio file.
You do not need to do any relaxation technique.

Just say to yourself, "I choose to go into my peace zone now," take a deep breath, and focus on this calmness and peace for a moment or two. Run the keyword you picked through your brain.

Say "Calm" "Relax" or "Peace" to yourself. If you can visualize, see something that is relaxing and peaceful to you. Imagine it in your brain as clearly as you can. Loosen up your muscles and relax.

This won't work spectacularly the first time you do it, but it works more strongly as you continue to do it and turn it into a habit. The more you go into the peace zone, the stronger the feeling becomes and the more control you have over the *feelings* of calmness and peace.

2. **Tell yourself you're entering the peace zone. Use the same steps as above and visualize if you can.** See a waterfall or the crystal blue clear waters of a Pacific island.

You control the way you feel by going into your "peace zone." Practicing this when you are not anxious makes it easier to do when you *are* feeling anxious. You can control and feel calmness if you gently keep doing this every day.

Calmness is not limited to one specific place. We can feel calmness anywhere, in whatever situation we find ourselves in.

Tell yourself to go into the "peace zone." As you start this, some days will work better than others, but continue patiently using your keyword and experience some calmness and peace.

You are turning this into a habit so that when you say "relax," you immediately feel more calm and peaceful, and you are reminded to slow down and take your time. Peaceful feelings grow stronger over time. Choose to move into the peace zone every day.

You see how "slow talk," "loosening up," "progressive muscle relaxation," and "the peace zone" all fit together. As you practice all of these slowing down methods, you will be growing a feeling of calmness and peace and turning it into a habit.

This calmness and peace is yours; it occurs in your brain. Accept it and enjoy it, and let it blossom and grow in your life. Calmness and peace replace anxiety and fear as you focus on your peace zone, and will win out as you make calmness into a habit.

I will use my keyword ("relax") to remind me to loosen up, relax, and slow down. I will take it easy on myself and focus on feeling calmness and peace.

Acceptance is an Active Experience
This is an Emotional Brain, "Peace Zone" Handout

I accept who I am.
I want to grow and learn new things.

I accept the good that's happening in my life. I am no longer fighting, battling, or struggling with anything.

As I accept this peace, I interrupt and interfere with my negative emotions. I accept my peace and calmness, because acceptance permits my calmness and peace to keep growing.

In acceptance there is peace and harmony. I am in the flow of the moment. I am present in the here and now.

I move out and ahead naturally. My attention is on the present. My focus is on the good and positive things that are happening to me today.

My brain moves in the direction that I want it to move in. It can move toward worry – or it can move toward peace. I deliberately choose peace.

Active acceptance helps me move toward calmness and peace.
I am in the flow of the moment as I accept.
I know that when I am in this flow I am moving in a positive direction.
My life unfolds neatly and naturally when I am in this peaceful flow.

As I stay focused in the present, I learn to actively accept more easily.
Active acceptance unleashes a great calming power.

I accept the peace, the tranquility, and the calmness.
I accept the present moment and the joys that are in it.
I accept that this peace is leading me in the right direction.
I sit back, loosen up, and let go of all my doubts and worries.
I accept this peaceful feeling and choose to let it do its work.

The peace inside this flow is very strong.
I focus on peace and feel it flowing through me.
It is an energizing, motivating, tranquil flow.
It helps me accept and live in the present moment.

My old worries are in the past.
They are gone. They are over. They are finished forever.
I am living in the present. I accept and dwell in the calmness of the present moment.
This calmness brings peace, power, and strength.
I accept this peace, power and strength.

There is no battle here.
There is no struggling here.
There is no fighting here.
Instead, I accept my peace and allow it to flow through me.

I have decided to move forward in life.
The old things in my past are in my past.
I will not go back to the trash dump and play around in the filth.

Instead, I gladly accept the peace, tranquility, and calmness that it brings.
I am OK in myself. I feel confident, calm, and assured.
My power and confidence come from my peace.

My peace grows stronger every day.
My focus is acceptance, on today, on my peace.
My attention is on the calmness of the present moment.
When I am in this flow of calmness, I feel peace and power. I accept this peace naturally.

Peace is a gift.
I don't have to earn it. I don't have to plead for it. I don't have to do anything but accept it.

Peace originates in my brain, and all human beings have the power to use their feeling of calmness and peace.

I accept peace because it is mine.
It is mine today – right this very moment.
In my peace, I feel the calmness moving me forward and upward.
I accept this peace and let it occur naturally.
This peace and this calmness are mine.
They have always been mine, and I accept them completely.
I accept and I grow.

It is simply a fact... a strong and powerful fact.

I accept these feelings of peace and calmness.

As a result, my whole life changes.

Seeing the Present
This is an emotional brain, "peace zone" handout

We have the power to live our own realities. Because we have free will, we can choose, pick options, open ourselves up to new experiences, stay where we are, or even limit ourselves.

We have control over all our own choices, because they are all internal choices. All of them exist inside our own brain.

I can choose to be free of the past.
I can choose to be free of my old limitations.
I can choose to be myself, a new self, a better self, a self not tied down to any feeling or emotion from my past.

I am not limited by my past, unless I choose to let it limit me.

Instead, I see myself moving ahead and forward. I see myself "taking the steps" of the present moment. I see each forward step as movement in the present moment.

The picture in my mind is peaceful and serene. I see myself growing happier and more content with each step I take.

As I choose to live in the present, I won't drag the past along behind me.

The past is gone, I release it, I set it free, and it has no hold on me today.

I see it floating away, disappearing into the clouds, and it sets me entirely free.

I am always free as I let go of the past. The old restrictions and limitations that try to tie me down are gone. I choose to live in the present moment, and I choose the new me, on this new day, in the new life I am creating for myself.

I close my eyes and see the present. The present is always free and boundless.

I am strong in the present moment. I am healthy in the present moment. My strength is in the present.

The present is my life. It does no good to think about the past or the future because they do not exist.

My focus is on – today – this very moment. I see myself, hands extended, accepting the present moment and all the joys within.

The present moment is my moment. It belongs to me. I see myself accepting the present. I reject the impossibilities of the past and the fears of the future. In the present, these realities do not exist. In the present, I am always free.

I live in the present moment. I make a choice to live happily and contentedly in the present moment.

The present always exists and I choose to live in the truth. The present is my reality and I choose the contentment, strength, and confidence of today.

As I focus more steadily on the present moment, I grow stronger and more at peace. The calmness overtakes me and I accept and enjoy it.

As my attention stays in the present, my peace, my strength, and my power increase. There is no going back for me. The victory is in the present. The victory is my calmness and peace. I choose to live in the present moment, where I can be happy and calm.

AT THE CROSSROADS
This is an emotional brain, "Peace Zone" Handout

As I stand at the crossroads,

Dozens of pathways lie before my eyes, each leading in a different direction.

I am confused and don't know which pathway to take.

At first, it seems overwhelming because there are so many choices I can make, and all the choices make it seem overwhelming.

What if I make the wrong choice? What if my decision leads me down the wrong road? What if I mess up my school, my career, my relationship, my family?

But then I catch myself. I know it can't be that difficult. I am starting to doubt and worry. Worry, doubt, and confusion will not allow me to make a rational decision about the direction I'm taking.

As I calm down and begin to feel a peace deep inside of me, my vision slowly changes.

I still see the pathways and the many roads that lie before me, but they don't look the same to me anymore. Something has changed. Something is different.

Some of the pathways have ugly weeds growing around them, and they narrow down into darker and darker lanes. I don't feel right about those roads.

Other roads are clearer and I can see farther, but they don't feel right to me either. I am not drawn to them. They do not make me feel peaceful or calm.

Something somewhere is out of focus, out of place.

And then – I catch myself again. This is good, I think.

I close my eyes, take a very deep breath, and accept the peace and the direction that is already there.

It is simply a matter of acceptance. I will accept the peace, the strength, and the confidence inside me.

As my eyes slowly open again, the pathways in front of me look very different again.

I see several pathways that look pleasant, good, and positive. It is life in the present moment and the wind, the fresh air, and the beautiful surroundings increase my feelings of calmness and peace.

Somehow, I know the old, ugly pathways are still in front of me, but I'm not focused on them anymore. I am calm… I am at peace.

But still, for a fleeting second, the old thoughts come back: "What if I make the wrong decision?"

Quickly and deliberately, and faster this time, I stop dead in my tracks. I know how to get in tune with my inner harmony and peace.

So, I accept and allow my peace to flow over me. I see myself covered over completely in this calm, refreshing feeling.

As I open my eyes again, the pathways in front of me unfold further, but one of them is shining and stands out from the rest. This road feels right to me. It feels better, more natural, and more safe. There are opportunities down this road, and I can sense that it will lead me in the right direction.

And, so I slowly step into this pathway, always aware of the fact that I can change my mind or take another path at any time that I want. I am never trapped when I walk down this kind of pathway and the peace is so strong and vibrant. The skies open up above me and the dawn of this beautiful brightness allows my vision to enlarge and expand.

As I walk farther along my pathway, I begin to feel even better. I am taking one step at a time and enjoy living in the present moment.

The farther I travel, the more serene and calming my pathway becomes. My mind is now more alert and clear. I hear beautiful sounds and see beautiful sights. Everything opens up for me very naturally. I accept this pathway because I choose to. I know and feel that it is the right way for me. It is a rational and healthy pathway and it is leading me forward, naturally and gently, into even better lands.

LETTING GO of the NEGATIVE PAST:
Embracing the Powerful and Positive Future

I accept myself for who I am.

I have many good, creative talents I can use to help others and myself.

That old, emotional baggage from the past can only drag me down, so I reject it.

I choose to live in the moment and be happy and content.

When I am happy in the present moment, it guarantees that my future will be happy.

I give up and set free all the negativity of the past, no matter how far down in my brain it is buried.

I accept myself for who I am, knowing that I am walking the road to becoming healthier.

Release your emotional baggage

Any thought, memory, or experience in the past that is weighing my brain down today and causing my progress to stall – I let it go, I set it free, I give it up.

I give up anything that is buried in my past that makes me unhappy today.

I take a deep breath, loosen up my muscles, feel the calmness and peace, and set free all the negative emotions from the past.

I release the negative feelings that I repressed in the past. I can see they only harm me.

I release them and let them go. I watch as they disappear completely into the air above me or into the ground beneath me.

Negative feelings and emotions can only weigh me down and cause me problems. So I choose to move forward with my life and not be weighed down by my past.

I release all the negative emotion of the past and I breathe in the positive power of my peacefulness.

I accept this peace. I accept this calmness.

I am free from the shame, embarrassment, and guilt of the past.

I fully release those negative emotions and set them free. I allow my mind to release them naturally.

I choose to move forward into my peace, my health, and my clarity of thought.

As I close my eyes, I can see my old negative feelings rise above me and disappear into the air.

No longer does shame, embarrassment or guilt bind me. No longer am I a captive of these negative emotions. All they do is hold me back, make me miserable, and make my thoughts confused and irrational.

I let these negative emotions from the past go. My mind is releasing them now this very moment. As I set them free, my mind feels more and more at peace.

I choose peace, tranquility, understanding, and confidence. I choose to grow strong and healthy. I let go of the shackles that have held me down for so very long.

I accept the good, the better, and the beautiful. I accept the rational truth that lies before me.

And so, I turn away from the old responses of the past, and again, I set them free. All the old negative emotions have no choice – they must go away. They cannot co-exist in my brain with peace and strength and confidence.

Shame, guilt, embarrassment, and feelings of failure are nothing more than ways to hold me back. I set them free. I release them. I let them go.

I accept myself and my healing. I allow my brain to work in a positive manner, for my good, and for my health.

My strength comes now, in the present, as I release all my negative emotions, and deliberately allow my mind to be saturated with rational, realistic, healthy emotions.

This feeling of peace and security is already inside me, and it will grow with time. I am in touch with my peace, my calmness, and my tranquility.

Inside my peace, there is healing and power. I accept these as part of my new life.

So I accept them: Peace, power, calmness, strength, clarity of mind, and purpose. They are mine. I own them.

Taking Responsibility and Making Choices

Every day, I am actively deciding to do things.
What I actively decide to do shapes my day.
What I actively decide to do today changes tomorrow.
What I actively decide to do today affects my entire future.

I am personally responsible for my own life and how it unfolds, with a rational and common sense understanding.
No one else can make these decisions and choices for me.
I have choices to make every moment of the day.

I can decide to be depressed because I am not yet where I want to be in life.
I can decide I am no good because I dropped out of college.
I can decide to be depressed because life hasn't turned out like I'd planned.
I can decide to have a bad day at work because every other day has been bad.

If I make these decisions, I can also make healthier decisions.
I have the power to make small decisions every day concerning my life.
These small decisions won't make a big difference today.
But these small decisions will literally change my entire life over time.

I have many more decisions than I ever thought possible.
I am responsible for today – I am responsible for this minute.
I can make healthy, positive decisions for myself and my future, or
I can make negative decisions that depress me, pull me down, and hold me stuck in my own tracks.

If I did it, I can undo it. No one else can do this for me.
I always have a choice. In fact, I always have choices.

But choices exist only in the present. I can decide to do something, to act, to be in a "good" mood; and I can do everything possible to bring this about.

Or, I can give up, give in to my depression, and wallow in the mud for another day. If I wallow in the mud enough, I will learn to enjoy it.

I need to take responsibility for my own life, grow wiser, and stop complaining. I have many choices I can make, and I make choices every day.

It is wiser for me to make healthy choices for myself in the present moment.

That is what will make my future work out.

Something You Should Think About:
Be Honest With Yourself

Do you realize your own value and worth as a person?

Look at what you're becoming. Look at the way you handle anxiety now. Look at the progress you've made. Look at all the things you've learned that will help you for the rest of your life.

Think about it. Be rational with yourself.

Anxiety causes people to de-value themselves and put themselves down. Do you still do that?

Do you give yourself rational credit for the positive steps you are making in moving your life forward? It's important you do that. All of us need to be accepting of ourselves and learn to like ourselves.

I accept because I know it's the right thing to do. It leads me towards my peaceful future.

Do you still see yourself as inferior to other people? You are not. Do you compare yourself to other people and think that all of them are somehow "better" than you? That is not true whatsoever. Nothing you do when making "comparisons" like this is valid or rational.

Within your brain lies the calmness and peace you will use for the rest of your life. Your calmness will be noticed by others and you will find yourself a positive role model for others in remaining calm and staying peaceful.

The days of being on "high alert" are over. **We can even respond to anxiety with calmness and peace, now that we know anxiety cannot harm us in any way.** Anxiety's days are numbered. Living in the present moment – and enjoying my calmness and peace – guarantees that.

How much automatic negative thinking are you still doing? Why are you still doing it? Are you catching it – labeling it – and turning the tables on it? Your thoughts are changing – notice this – and your thought processes are different now than they were before.

This change in what you believe is a *permanent* change with permanent repercussions. Many people with anxiety problems have positive and caring personalities. This may be because of all the suffering we have endured and our ability to empathize with others.

It is anxiety that hides, blocks, restricts, and keeps our "true" personalities from emerging.

Your own value and worth as a human being are eminently more important than you think.

Maybe you are not opening up your mind to your own value and worth in this world. Maybe you do not realize that you have a very positive contribution to make to the people you will meet and know during your lifetime.

Maybe you haven't even thought about any of this before.

So that is why I want to say this: You should think about your value and worth as a human being.

You have a lot to give to other people, as you continue to overcome social anxiety and allow your true self to emerge.

As you make progress, it becomes easier to see, feel, and act like who you truly are.

Improving our Public Speaking, Presentations, and Talks

Interestingly enough, 93% of the population, according to the latest data, detest public speaking and will avoid it at all costs. What this means, of course, is that you are already AHEAD of the average person and you are already doing more than what the "general public" does.

Without taking away any of this good progress you have already made, how can we hierarchically (step by step) improve on our speaking skills, be it as a public speaker, or just when we're talking one on one with other people?

Let's not handle this the Toastmaster way and "beep" you every time you make a mistake. We don't need to focus negatively on little mistakes.

Although we'll make mistakes, just catch it, and plan to do better next time. Don't dwell on a small mistake.

Let's look at this more realistically. These are simply steps – if you are *patient* with yourself, you can improve your speech (talk) even further.

Key: We are on a hierarchy. Your attempts are the victory. You will make mistakes, like everyone else. So what? The only way to reach our goal is by making mistakes. Then, we stay patient with ourselves as we learn from our mistakes.

Mistakes are good things because we can discover how to be better at something because of what we've learned. When you realize you're saying "umm" too much, be encouraged, note it, and try to do better next time.

Be patient with yourself, congratulate yourself for your attempts, and continue to do better.

Here are several things you may have noticed:

Phrases or sounds that are not words that we use to tie our thoughts together or that we say when we are "reaching" for our next thought. These are sounds such as such as "Umm…" "uh…" or "Uhhh…"

When you notice yourself doing this, note it, and plan to do better next time. Gradually eliminate the excess sounds that don't need to be there.

We all do this type of thing when we're speaking, but gradually eliminating these sounds from your speaking will do wonders. People listen and pay attention to you more if you sound more coherent and have less of these sounds to fill empty space. This is not simply applicable to business situations; it is applicable to everything you say in any form of human interaction.

Do not pressure yourself with this and do not beat yourself up. Recognize your mistakes, be happy you recognize them, and then it becomes easier to slowly and gradually stop making sounds or phrases that are not needed.

Another way of making our speaking better is by avoiding apologetic or hesitant words.

Those of us with anxiety are prone to making tentative or hesitant remarks because it seems difficult for us to just "step out there," and take a chance. We've been avoiding all our lives.

For example, we sometimes say "Well, I'm not sure of the date (or the place) (or the person)…" This just wastes time and takes away from your message. If you don't know the date, time, or person – don't mention it. Instead, eliminate these tentative words from your talk. You don't need to make excuses for yourself.

Another example: "I can't remember exactly how it happened, but…" A statement like this is not needed. It is best to eliminate it and continue with your talk.

No one can remember everything in detail. You are not "lying" just because you cannot remember a date, a name, or a specific detail. Allow yourself to generalize when necessary, because it gets your story across better to other people.

Extraneous sentences

Many times those of us with anxiety add sentences that are not necessary, because we are thinking in such detail and we want to be accurate – we don't want to be proven wrong or have someone think we are wrong. This is something we do because of our fear of disapproval.

If a sentence is not necessary – just leave it out, and go on.

It is always best to just go on. Catch yourself if you are being tentative or hesitant, but don't apologize for it. Just note it and try to do better next time. And continue on… As you continue on, it becomes easier for your mind to see what needs to be said and what doesn't.

Handle this in a nice, gentle, way… and your speaking will improve, you will be more "effective" when you talk, and people will listen to you more closely.

The *"Key"* Key: You are being proactive by working on this slowly. You will make mistakes – you can't get better unless you make mistakes – and handling the mistakes with patience and a willingness to do better, keeps you moving forward toward reaching your goal.

You never, under any circumstances, have a rational right to beat yourself up.

Continue being proactive. Realize that you have won this battle so long as you're patient and make changes when you notice them. It's a mistake to fear mistakes. Making mistakes is the only way people make progress. Mistakes are good things because they show us what we need to do to get better.

The Perfectionism Pit

Seeking perfection only leads to frustration and defeat.
Why should I expect perfection? Why should I set myself up for frustration and defeat?

Instead, I will do my best, and then move forward. I can never make anything "perfect."

I can do the best I can. That is all I can ever do – and it is always enough.
If I search for perfection, I will never find it. It will always elude me. I will be trapped in anxiety and defeat.

If I try to be perfect, the ANTs thoughts and feelings will cause me stress, doubt, confusion, and turmoil.

I choose to slow down, reach my peace zone, get clarity of mind, and do what I can do.

That is always good enough. I don't need to push for the impossible. I will do my best and my best is good enough.

Human beings are never "perfect." It is a futile, impossible task to even attempt. All I can do is my best – and my best is good enough.
As I live in my peace zone, I realize that my mind can be clear, I can do what I need to do, and then I can move forward.

I move on and I move forward because I did what I could. I did my best under the circumstances. That is more than good enough.

I make mistakes like everyone else. It's no big deal. It proves that I'm human. It does no good to try to be Superman.

The more I pressure myself into doing a perfect job, the more problems I cause for myself.

So, I deliberately slow down, relax, calm myself, and accept the peace and strength that belongs to me.

Perfectionism leads to negative, anxious thoughts and emotions. Trying to be perfect is a big ANT. It is doomed to failure and it will make me an unhappy person.

Instead, I choose to go with the truth. I choose reality. I can do what I can do. And that is enough. I can gently, nicely, and peaceably move on.

I am not perfect. No one is perfect. It does no good to try to be perfect. I clear out my mind, settle myself down, and do what I am capable of doing. There is strength and power in this peace.

If I do what I am capable of doing, that is enough, and I can move on.
Trying to be the best at something is competitive, comparative, and fuels ANTs thinking.

I choose the path of acceptance and calmness. By choosing this pathway, I feel better, get more quality work done, and am able to move on and move forward.

My peace and my calmness are stronger than my old perfectionism.

I am a human being and I can't expect and seek after perfection. I can accept peace, calmness, and strength. They allow me to do what needs to be done in a time-efficient manner.

I deliberately reject the striving, pressuring feelings. I deliberately accept my calmness, my peace, and my progress.

I am moving ahead in the right manner. I accept my strengths and limitations.

I am moving ahead into my peace zone. I will get more done by living in my peace and my strength.

I accept this positive emotion and I move on in calmness and in confidence. I am whole.

Eliminating Fear and Anxiety Permanently
Taking the Last Step

To eliminate our fears and anxieties permanently, we need to take one more proactive step. We can't sit around, enjoy our progress, and vegetate. If we remain quiet and simply defend ourselves from anxiety, we won't have the opportunity to take the most proactive step of all.

Even when we've fully learned to respond to anxiety with calmness, there is one more step we need to take so that this major change in our life is permanent, and we are an entirely new person.

Because we can see and believe things rationally now, we can act on any situation, take the initiative with it, and learn to enjoy events, experiences, and situations. Living life can be an exciting event, and now that we're no longer tied down to anxiety's apron strings, we can act on life and be willing, even desirous, to engage in new activities, some of which will become fun, enjoyable and entertaining to us.

Life is motivating and fun and can be lived in a better way than we've experienced in the past. You are now in control of your own life and you make your own decisions, no longer based on anxiety, but based on what you *want* to do and what you find enjoyable in life.

*SPECIAL NOTE: If what we're talking about sounds "too fast" or too positive at this point, it's good to go back in the series and review prior therapy sessions to make sure that you have carried out all the concepts and reinforced them enough times. Reviewing, refreshing yourself with what is rational, and reinforcing all the cognitive therapy is vital in having it work for us. It's tough breaking old thinking habits, and you need to patiently stick with it, in the way that has been explained, until your new rational thoughts become your automatic thinking.

In the space of twenty four weeks or so, even if you have been consistent with your 30 minutes a day practice, the brain can't process everything you've done well enough to achieve the progress I'm talking about today. So this is a good time to go back and thoroughly review the cognitive strategies you've learned and then act on them to make sure they are at a foundational level in your brain. Review and repetition is necessary for all the strategies to fully work.

This handout starts with the premise that you are rational now, that you have acted against anxiety, and put the strategies into place in your life. Now, you're ready for this one last action that will make anxiety and fear remnants of the past.

This final step – which makes overcoming social anxiety permanent – is a step that needs to be repeated and reinforced like everything else. It is the final step, however, and it will be easier to you to put into place than any of the steps you have taken in the past.

We've used the "making a presentation" example before, so let's use this example again. Let's make it crystal clear and then and add the final step to it. This is something that is only possible because you have made progress in working through all the prior sessions.

If the boss just told me I need to give a presentation next week, I react to this news calmly and peaceably and tell myself the truth:

- ➢ "Presentations don't scare me as they used to. Last time I gave one I received some positive feedback from other people. I know they meant what they said and they weren't lying to me. What they said was genuine. Because of their feedback, I understand that when I give a presentation, I must do an OK job at it. There is nothing for me to worry about. In fact, based upon what I know and what I've been told, I *expect* to do a good job when I make my presentation next week."

- ➢ I have acted proactively by cooperating with my rational thinking and agreeing with it. It is rational to believe external sources rather than my old internal feelings. When I present next Tuesday, what I expect to happen, happens.

- ➤ I notice all this, give the presentation, and listen to the comments other people make to me.

- ➤ Then, I take it one step further. I think about how I can do an even better job next time.

- ➤ Since public speaking is something I do relatively well – many people have told me that – then maybe it's something I'm beginning to enjoy. I'm good at it, and I have the desire to do a better job next time.

Taking this last step has changed the brain entirely – relative to social anxiety. We are no longer wired to be anxious and fearful. Now, our response to life is calmness and peacefulness. We no longer think irrationally and act on our cognitively-distorted brain. We are out of anxiety's grip altogether, and we're looking forward to the next presentation and how to do an even better job at it.

This action on our part opens the door of creativity, and we throw our passion into it. We don't stop when we learn to stop having anxiety. We take it one step further, and act on it, particularly if it interests us, or if we want to do it.

In the past, I hated meeting new people.
Now I've learned to enjoy it.
In the past, I avoided social situations.
Now I look forward to them and seek them out.

The end result is that I have no anxiety about public presentations, even if there are 100 people in the audience, because it's only more people. I already know how people respond to my presentations. They respond in the same way that others have in the past. There is no legitimate reason for me to worry or doubt myself.

I have a deep, complete understanding of what "no big deal" means.

Taking one more proactive step allows us to be permanently successful. Not only are we not anxious, we are learning to like doing things that we've never done before.

We're open to new experiences and new outcomes. We look forward to getting out of bed in the morning, and doing things during the day that are novel, interesting, exciting, and add motivation to life.

We stay proactive and positive. By acting on the situations in life, I can look forward to positive things occurring. I'm not held down by the anxiety of the past. That's all behind me now as I act on what I know is rational.

I do new things and I learn that some of them are enjoyable and fun. They aren't dreadful and awful like I used to believe.

My brain has entirely changed. Now I take the initiative and find new, exciting things to do. Anxiety has no hold on me anymore. When I start taking the initiative and doing what I know is rational, I continue to find that situations in life can be interesting and enjoyable.

When I take another step, I find something else that motivates me to enjoy life. I like being around other people and interacting with them. I expect it to turn out well, and it does.

You are letting **optimism** take control of your life.

There are a lot of things we find interesting and enjoyable and now we're finding and doing them. Instead of being inside our brains, we're on the outside actually living. We're living life and enjoying the ride.

By taking this last step and acting on what you know is true, your expectations are grounded in fact.

> ➢ **My expectations become reality as I'm willing to act on them. As I act on them, what I expected to happen, happened, and a whole new world is in front of me. Now I view, see, and think rationally, and I do something about it as a result.**

There's nothing to hold me back any longer.

> ➢ **I know what's true and I want to keep moving on. There is optimism for the future, and I am relieved that my dark days are over. I don't think about them. There are too many good, positive, and fun things to do instead.**

The Paradox of the Rain

They say that into every life some rain must fall...
What they say is true, but they never tell you that rain can be seen as either a blessing or a curse, and it is up to me to determine which way I will see it.

Rain is relaxing, soothing, invigorating, and energizing, and it sets the cycle of growth in motion.

There can be no growth without the rain.

So even though the rain may be unpleasant for a while, it is never my enemy. It is always my friend.

I am my own worst enemy if I view the rain as being a curse.
In reality, the rain is not a curse. It is a blessing. It is necessary for my growth... a healthy, invigorating, motivating growth and healing.

The paradox of the rain is that, in order for it to be a blessing, I must recognize and accept it as a blessing.

The rain may be unwelcome and uncomfortable at times, but it is also preparing me for the growth that is to come.

The rain may be unpleasant, but eventually its drops flow down deeply into the earth to be able to produce a beautiful crop.

It all depends on the way I choose to see it.
The way I choose to see it affects my whole attitude and life.
Accepting the rain for the blessing it will become allows my progress in the present to proceed.

Rain always brings growth. It always brings healing.
I am guaranteed of that.
The paradox of the rain is that for the rain to bring me growth and healing, I must accept it.

As I accept it, my attitude and perspective begin to change.

Rain brings wonderful changes if it is allowed to accomplish its purpose.
Many people curse the rain and grow bitter against it.
These are people who never overcome their problems and never grow in their lives.

The flower accepts the storm because it knows it will be watered.
If the flower is watered, it will grow and blossom into something vibrant and beautiful.

My growth and blossoming is at hand. I accept it now and gladly choose to move forward.

Keep the Momentum Going and Do Not Give Up
Staying on Track

Keep on going… keep practicing… the cognitive therapy needs to be rooted in the brain so deeply that **you could not forget it even if you tried.**

A more valid statement could not be made.

There is no pill, no injection, no magic wand, and no operation that can help you overcome social anxiety.

And setbacks do happen to us all… it is how we handle the setbacks that makes all the difference.

It is your brain – your thinking habits, patterns, and beliefs – that must be permanently changed.

Do not give up when times get difficult. They get difficult for all of us. Keep going even when you feel you are not making progress.

You know by now that your feelings can be big liars and, if you go along with irrational feelings, you'll be down and depressed for days.

Even if it feels like the right thing to do, **do not go along with your irrational feelings.** Always choose your rational feelings – calmness, reflection, relaxation, peace.

Your rational feelings are always right and always lead you in the right direction. Your negative emotions are always wrong and lead you back into "Anxiety Land."

By this time, you should know that going along with your irrational emotions is a ticket to anxiety and depression. Deliberately choose your rational thinking, and deliberately dismiss your emotional thinking. Your negative emotions are wrong –

they are not rational – and going along with them will make you miserable, and stop your progress.

When you fall, pick yourself up, dust yourself off, and move forward – go along with your rational thinking. Listen to your brain, and not to your emotions.

As long as you continue to move on, you will make it to your destination. It is only people who fall and stay fallen who get stuck and do not reach their goals.

So, please – keep on going and do not give up. You know that overcoming social anxiety takes patience and time because you are breaking long-held, irrational thinking habits.

You're breaking up, interrupting, and changing these old, long-held irrational thoughts and beliefs. Keep on breaking up these irrational thoughts and feelings until they are gone for good.

When that last restriction that anxiety causes melts away, you are free to live the kind of life you want. You will be very happy that you kept on going – even when the times were tough.

Everyone with social anxiety can get better. Just keep moving on, applying the cognitive solutions to situations in your daily life.

The only people who fail are ones that give up. So, please don't give up. Keep going, keep putting the strategies into practice – be proactive: act on life instead of reacting to it.

Keep on going and do not give up.

Do these two things and social anxiety will be a thing of the past. You will have an entirely new life ahead of you, filled with optimism, new discoveries, and new interpersonal relationships.

If you encounter a problem along the way, you always have the cognitive strategies, in writing, that you can refer back to. This will keep you on track no matter where you are in your progress. The solutions to social anxiety are all there, and you have access to every single one of them.

Just because you finished the series, doesn't mean your brain has had the time to change completely. Let me encourage you to go back and go over the series again, because you'll be surprised at the new things you pick up when you review it the second time.

Over the past fifteen years, we've had international groups of people come to the Social Anxiety Institute, and the one thing that really helps is that these people have gone over the entire series three, four, five, six times. **Every time they go through it, they see something that they missed before.**

It's gratifying to hear them realize this, and to realize that they are getting better and better. Noticing the material you missed, and putting it into place in your life by acting on it, is the way to keep the momentum going and to continue making progress.

They also realize that the sky's the limit. They've decided to keep on putting the strategies into practice until they are automatically doing them. Then there will be no more irrational anxiety left.

You are always making progress, and you will reach your goal of being anxiety-free, as the strategies, thoughts and beliefs become permanent and automatic.

I suspect that the look-around technique is automatic for you now, just as all the other cognitive strategies will become automatic when you've reinforced them enough. The brain changes every time you put a strategy into place, and that puts you one step closer to overcoming social anxiety completely.

At this point, keep on going with your rational thoughts and beliefs. Your negative emotions may try to trip you up, because ANTs are sneaky, but you can see now that going along with your rational emotions and your rational thoughts is the healthiest alternative, and will move you along the path to overcoming social anxiety altogether.

Reinforce any cognitive strategy that is not thoroughly grounded in your brain. Review and implement it in the way that is talked about in the session.

If you just keep on going and do not give up, you will reach that goal of overcoming social anxiety for good. You'll have an entirely new life in front of you.

You have changed your brain, and now you have a life that is no longer restricted by social anxiety.

This book of handouts accompanies the audio and video series *"Overcoming Social Anxiety: Step by Step"* by Dr. Thomas A. Richards and is not meant to be a book separate from the entire program. This book works in conjunction with the audio and video components of the therapy series.

Where to go for more information:

http://socialanxietyinstitute.org

https://members.socialanxietyinstitute.org

https://socialanxietyinstitute.org/overcoming-social-anxiety-experiences

The interactive forum can be found at:

http://forum.socialanxietyinstitute.org/

A section of the forum is for public questions and information. The private area of the forum is for use by people working on the therapy series "Overcoming Social Anxiety: Step By Step."

Other sources of information about anxiety:

http://anxietynetwork.com
Current information about panic disorder and generalized anxiety disorder can be found on this site.

http://socialphobia.org
Non-profit organization to assist people with social anxiety disorder.

About Dr. Thomas A. Richards
and the Social Anxiety Institute

Dr. Thomas A. Richards, a licensed psychologist, is director of the Social Anxiety Institute in Phoenix. He is now in his twentieth year of helping people overcome social anxiety, by use of rational cognitive-behavioral therapy. He has seen people from all over the world and had the opportunity to work with them directly, individually and through social anxiety CBT groups.

The Social Anxiety Institute has become international as twenty-five percent of the people seen are from outside the United States.

Dr. Richards has spoken at conferences all over the United States about social anxiety, always with an emphasis on helping people overcome it. In addition, he was asked by many operating groups to help, speak, and answer questions about the **Overcoming Social Anxiety: Step by Step** program. He has spent many days with therapy groups throughout the country, helping the group leaders become more effective at their job.

He received both the M.A. and Ph.D. degrees in psychology from **Arizona State University**. After receiving his doctoral degree, Dr. Richards served at several universities throughout the U.S. in the psychological field. During this time, he won several awards for teaching and instructional excellence, and, among other honors, was chosen outstanding professor of the year. He left academics in the early 1990s to open a private psychological practice, which later turned into the Social Anxiety Institute.

He founded the **Anxiety Clinic of Arizona** in September, 1994, and treated people with panic disorder, generalized anxiety disorder, and social anxiety disorder. The first social anxiety groups occurred at this time and have continued through the present day. As the clinic reputation grew, Dr. Richards and staff made the decision to focus entirely on social anxiety disorder, as there was virtually no help for this problem anyplace in the world. **The Social Anxiety Institute** was officially founded in 1999, as a way to indicate to everyone that the institution treated and worked with people who had social anxiety disorder only. Prior to the official re-naming and incorporation, Dr. Richards had already begun working solely with social anxiety people. The first international group happened accidentally in 1998, but within several weeks of agreeing to do it, the first "international" group was in operation.

As the Social Anxiety Institute grew, he established the first web site on the internet entirely dedicated to social anxiety. In 1999, the **Social Anxiety Institute website** became active and continues to this day. It was totally updated and revised at the beginning of 2013, and has increased its presence on the internet as a source for information and treatment of social anxiety disorder. As a result of his prior experience dealing with other anxiety disorders, he had written and published the first website that dealt solely with all the anxiety disorders. **The Anxiety Network** became operational in 1995, and continues to this day, reaching upwards of 35,000 people a month.

Today, Dr. Richards is seen as one of the leading clinical authorities on social anxiety disorder, due to the international reputation of the Social Anxiety Institute and the fact that he has seen more patients with social anxiety disorder than any other therapist or psychologist in practice. People travel to SAI from every corner of the world because adequate treatment for social anxiety disorder does not yet exist. The **international program** at the Social Anxiety Institute has been operating continuously since 1998. The treatment programs at the Social Anxiety Institute are the most comprehensive and therapeutic programs in the world.

The **weekly all-day Saturday programs** continue to run, and the program has grown exponentially since 1994. The current Saturday group is made up of people from all over the United States – people who have moved here to receive treatment, as treatment for social anxiety virtually does not exist in the U.S. yet. In the "local" group, typically half our members come from people from other states who moved here for cognitive-behavioral treatment. The Social Anxiety Institute has become a national and international treatment center.

In addition to speaking engagements, Dr. Richards has organized and run large conferences about social anxiety disorder throughout the country.

At present, he and his team are working on several other projects to provide added therapy assistance to people who cannot make it to the Social Anxiety Institute for any of its programs.

Made in the USA
Lexington, KY
06 August 2015